What God Can Do...

With a Surrendered Life

Diane Profet

Contents

My Life...

My life has been a beautiful puzzle created and fit together by the Father Himself. Every single thing that has happened was orchestrated by God for His purpose and His glory. My life is meant to bring about the beauty of God. I was created to praise Him every minute I breathe the breath of life. All my days I will tell of the excellent things He has done in and through me.

May you read these words and feel encouraged and inspired by my life.

"I will speak of Your splendor and glorious majesty and Your wonderful works."

— Psalm 145:5 CSB

Chapter 1
Childhood

To understand all that God has done, we must start at the beginning. My childhood was met with adversity, hardships, and trials. Abandonment plagued my life as a child.

My American dad met my Mexican mother in Mexico, and dad couldn't speak Spanish, and mother spoke broken English. But they married and began a life together, first in Mexico, and after my sister was born, in California. Apparently at that time in America, they did not  want you to teach your native language to your children, or so my mother was told by the school officials where my older sister had begun school, who spoke in Spanglish, a mix of Spanish and English. "You're in

America, don't speak Spanish to your kids" said the school officials. So, my mother had to improve her English and from then on tried to speak to us only in English.

Together, my parents had four children: my sister Judy was the oldest, then Harvey, then myself, and then my brother Steven.

Growing up, my mother spoke English with my siblings and myself. The only time she didn't speak English was when she was upset and then she'd would only speak her native Spanish. . When she was upset, we knew it, and somehow, we understood every Spanish word.

MY MOTHER

Chapter 2
My Mother

My mother, Maria Del Carmen, was born and raised in Acaponeta, Nayarit, Mexico and went through trials and tragedies before I was born. She was a twin, but her sibling died at birth. Many years later, my mother also miscarried twins.

I never met my mother's mother or father. My grandmother and her husband had eight children, but her husband was tragically kicked by a horse and bled to death. All at once my grandmother was left raising eight children by herself and living on a ranch. Not long after, she got involved with a married man (who was the father of my mother), and my mother was her ninth child. However, this man's jealous wife was out to kill both my mother and my grandmother.

My grandmother died when my mother was only eight months old. It appeared to be a deliberate act—some believe she may have been poisoned.

My mother was Catholic, and she knew about the Lord. I really do think she gave her heart to Him. At an early age my mother fell in love and decided to marry. She told me once that she never had a happy life due to trauma and her health issues (like her terrible migraines that would put her in bed for many days). She was ready to find her happiness and marry the man she loved. However, her older sisters disapproved of him and didn't want her to marry him, so they moved her away from that part of Mexico. Many, many years later, they got back in touch with each other. She was so excited to be back together and marry him, but before they could marry, he had a heart attack and died. She was left devastated and, again, unmarried.

My mother told me about her father, my grandfather, who I never met. He was the president of all the ranches, and his brother was the ambassador of Mexico. As a child she was never poor. When she needed anything, she would just use credit at the stores by telling them her name, and her father would pay for it. Every store knew him - he was very wealthy. My mother said she never knew then what it was to want anything.

After my grandfather died, my mother had a very hard life. When she was a teenager, a hitman came to her and said, "If you pay me more, I won't kill you." Her life had been so sad that she just said, "Do it." The hitman started shaking, then ran away. Soon after, my mother left that part of Mexico to get away from all the pain and trouble she had been through.

Many years later, my grandfather had willed his whole ranch over to my mom, but mother told me that she just signed it over to her father's sons, her half-brothers, who had worked the ranch for years.

I remember my mother cooking. She would make homemade tortillas; she would make a whole bunch of beans and rice. (I didn't know what vegetables were.) I would go to the grocery store and see cauliflower and thought it was processed flowers! It seems silly, but the first time I saw broccoli I really didn't know what it was; I couldn't figure it out. But when I was 16, I went to a party, and they had a vegetable platter and that's when I experienced eating vegetables for the first time. Whenever I saved money, I would buy vegetables because I didn't really care for sweets. I learned how to steam them and how to put butter in them - they tasted so good! I just enjoyed them so much. It was only when I went to Sommer Haven Ranch and met Sister Agnes, that I learned about spinach and all the different types of vegetables.

MY FATHER

Chapter 3
My Father

My mother moved from deeper South in Mexico to the border area near Arizona where a lot of her half-siblings lived and that's where she met my father. My dad, Monnie Curtis Watson, was about 45 and my mother was 19 when they got together. She might have been looking for a father figure when my dad came into her life.

My dad was born in Texas, but was living in Calexico, California and owned a lumber company that was transporting lumber from Calexico to San Luis, Mexico, right across the border from Arizona where mother lived. He had been previously married and had several children, all of whom were older than my mom. Dad and mother married and my sister, their first child, was born in Mexico in 1958. Shortly afterward though, dad and mother moved to Victorville, California to start a new life. The town was small back then in the early sixties when I was born, having only one grocery store, but grew quite a bit by the time I left home in 1981.

I only remember a few things about my dad. One was that he had dandruff, and he would sit in the chair and pay me a quarter to comb it out. Another time I remember was when my mother had asked my dad to pick up tamales at a Mexican restaurant. He brought them home, but they didn't give us the correct amount. I was crying because I wanted my extra tamales. But dad got so upset, he said, "You better cram that down your mouth." He even told me that I better do it very quickly.

My mother told me a story that dad had told her about his service in the military, in World War II. My dad was on a Navy ship and was a very good anti-aircraft gunner and was at that position when his ship was hit by gunfire from a Japanese airplane. My dad got shot but the wound didn't immobilize him, so after getting bandaged, he was put right back out on his gun because he was so good.

The Japanese attacks had knocked out all the ship's systems - no power, propulsion or communication – and they were just drifting out somewhere in the Pacific Ocean. Their food and water were nearly gone, and I recall mother saying that they knew they were goners because the ammunition was just about out, and they were still having to fend off Japanese planes. Then, like a miracle, they saw a military plane with a white star painted under its wing - a United States plane had located them! Other U.S. planes then came and dropped supplies. All the ship's crew got on their knees to thank God that their lives were saved because they had been so close to death.

In my early childhood, my father owned a roofing company in Victorville and had a wholesale company that he called Maria Wholesale. Dad had done a roofing job for the nearby George Air Force Base but installed the wrong material, and the military base refused to pay him for the job. At this point my dad went bankrupt and he already owed the IRS so much money, he just decided to leave us and disappear where the IRS couldn't catch up to him. These are some things I learned about my father and even now, I wish I could know more.

My father left our family when I was 6 years old. I remember that day, dad was recovering from hernia surgery but packed and loaded his suitcase anyway and said he was leaving. My brother sneaked into the car and tried to hide so he could go with him, but dad took him out of the car and said goodbye to us. He gave my mother $200 and then told my 8-year-old brother that he was now the man of the house and left in our family car. We never saw him again. We never knew or heard for years if he was alive or dead; we didn't know what had happened. My father never again communicated with us; never called, never sent a letter, nothing. My mother figured that he thought we would be better off if he didn't come around because the IRS might be looking for him. Maybe he didn't think he could give us a future.

Anyway, when dad left us, the bank came to repossess most of everything that we had, even our house. The gentleman from the bank felt sorry for my mother, so he said, "You can keep the truck." Besides the old truck, they let us keep a few furniture items and some odds and ends.

We then had to move from the nicer part of Victorville, into a very poor part of town. In our new neighborhood, I remember seeing poop on walls and cockroaches in shoes. My mother had a Mexican friend who rented us a house that was in the ghetto, and I would come home and see my mother's eyes so swollen from crying. She applied for welfare because that was the only way we could survive. I remember the joy of when we would go pick up our food commodities - my favorite was canned meat. We used it to make chicken and beef tacos and then we would get the cheese to add to it.

At that time, my mother would clean houses and iron clothes to make a little bit of money. She did get a job at Motel 6, but she had a hernia and would also get very bad migraine headaches that would put her in bed for a week, and we couldn't make any noise, and she couldn't be in any light.

Back then, as a child, whenever I thought about my dad, I just thought he was a hobo out there somewhere. I would always look at homeless men wondering if maybe it was my dad. Years later we found out that dad had died, and it actually brought relief, like, okay, I know where dad's at now.

My dad died in 1975 when I was 13 years old and then I knew he was gone for good - it was a day I would never forget. A relative sent us a newspaper article describing my dad's death on a main highway near El Centro, California with a photo of dad's glasses on the roadside with a chalked circle drawn around them. I still remember my dad's glasses, you know, those were the glasses he always wore.

Dad had been killed by a car while walking across the road near his fruit stand. My mother and all of us kids just cried and cried when we received the news, I felt so numb. I thought back to the day dad left us, seven years prior, the day I last saw him. My younger brother was only a toddler when dad left home and had no recollection of him, but my sister, who was nine, retained vivid memories of him.

Many years later she felt a strong urge to find dad's grave. She researched and found out dad was buried in a cemetery in El Centro and went there to tell him that she forgave him for leaving her and our family. At the cemetery, my sister had no idea which of the thousands was dad's grave. Out of nowhere, a young man appeared and asked if she needed help. My sister told him she was looking for her dad's grave and the man asked for his name. She told him and immediately he replied "Oh, come, he's buried over here." He brought my sister directly to dad's grave and when she turned around to thank the man he was gone – he had vanished in a large wide-open cemetery. She figured it was an angel.

Last Family Photo

My mother went to file claims after dad died to receive benefits because dad had been a veteran. They said, "Oh, you're the real wife." Apparently, dad had remarried illegally, and the illegally married wife had also tried to claim benefits but knew nothing of my dad's past. My mother, however, knew everything about dad and correctly answered every question that the Veteran's Administration people asked her, and she was awarded dad's benefits. She hadn't divorced dad nor remarried. We were so happy with his benefits because we could finally get adequate clothes and have more than just two sets of clothing.

I still think about when my father passed away. I pray

that he went to be with the Lord. You never know what happens in the final moments of someone's life.

When I was 16, I found a Bible and said, "Mom, what's this?" She replied, "That was your dad's Bible, he was Methodist." And she said that he would always say, "You've taken the children to the Catholic Church, but two of my children will serve the Lord."

A father of the fatherless and a judge for the widows, is God in His holy habitation.

— Psalm 68:5

Chapter 4

School Days and My Family

School... I think I had a mental block, maybe because of trauma as a child.

At school I was always in special classes, including speech classes, because my mom's first language was Spanish and I mixed up some Spanish with English and with mispronounced English. There were a lot of words I couldn't say correctly because I learned how to pronounce words the way mother said them—and she didn't

As a teen with my dog

pronounce them correctly. So, that's the way I would say it. It just seemed like I had difficulty, like a mental block. There were programs they had for children that were for reading disabilities, spelling, speech, and everything you could think of.

Life was different for me for some reason, more than my brothers and my sisters; I don't know why. I remember my mother saying, "I wish you were never born." "I never wanted you." "I never wanted a girl." Now, I think back and ask myself, what did she go through as a woman and as a young girl? But as a child, when you hear those words, you feel rejection. You can only see things right at the moment and not what God has for you in the future.

My brother Harvey was very abusive to me and was the leader of a gang. He was a year and three months older than I and would do things to me like cut my hair and put gum in my hair. If I was watching the TV, he would come and change the channel - it was just awful. Anything that would torment me, he would do it. Sometimes, when he came home, he would be high from sniffing paint. He would come home high, at two or three in the morning. I remember him banging on the walls saying, "I'm going to kill you. I'm going to kill you." He would yell and yell. It was terrifying. Perhaps it was just the devil who wanted to destroy me.

My brother Steven was about five or six years younger than me, and because of that age gap, we were never very close. I had already left home by the time he was growing up, so we didn't really grow up together. He was born just before our father left—he never got to know him.

Steven had quite a personality! We would laugh at him because my mother would have to hide the Twinkies which he loved to eat! He was saved at a young age and felt called to be a youth pastor. So, he went to the Assemblies of God college, graduated and became a youth pastor, and now he's a senior pastor of a church in McKinney, Texas and is also the baseball coach of the Assemblies of God University in Texas.

My sister Judy was very bright, and she achieved a lot. She eventually became a teacher—things always seemed to come easily for her. Even if I studied and studied for a test, I would fail it. Studying, speech, and math were so challenging for me.

My mother would never let me spend the night at someone's house. She was very protective in that way. One night, I think I was 14, she said I could spend the night at an elderly woman's house, who was a friend. That night, the gangs shot at our house and blew out the big front window right above the couch where I always slept. I could have been injured but God protected me - His hand was on me even then. At the time, I didn't see it like that. I didn't thank God and say, "Wow. You protected me." I slept on the couch because my brother had kicked me out of my room so he could put his girlfriend there. My brother, however, is proof that God can take sinners and redeem them.

When I was at Sommer Haven Ranch, I remember we would pray and intercede for him. We never knew but we would pray and intercede, and God always intervened. God knows your prayers before you even utter a word.

One time in Mexico, when my husband and I were missionaries living near San Quintin, Baja California, the Lord burdened my husband and I to came back to the Mission Center at Sommer Haven Ranch. I was not there even an hour, and we received a call from a family member, and they said, "Your brother's not going to make it, he's in a coma right now because of an overdose." I remember my husband, Jamie, and I going there and praying for my brother, and the Lord brought him back to life. So many times, we prayed and interceded, and God intervened.

Another time he even locked himself in the trunk of a car. He didn't want to live. We thought the spirit of suicide had come over him. At the time, I was at our new ministry center, and I remember being in the kitchen. Suddenly I felt something in my heart, and I said, "I have to go." I went to my home, and I began to travail, fighting against the spirit of death. They had not told me that my brother was missing, even though they had a police helicopter out looking for him. At the time of our prayer and intercession, his wife went out to the car and saw it barely move. Harvey had locked himself in the trunk, but God spared his life.

"...A prayer of a righteous person, when it is
brought about, can accomplish much."

— James 5:16 NASB

Once, I said to my brother, "You know, God saved your
life so many times through prayer and intercession. Why
don't you give your life to God?" Harvey said, "I'm not
ready to give Him my life." Just a few months after the
trunk incident, he called me and said, "Diane, I received
Christ in my life. I don't know why it took me so long."
Soon afterwards my husband, children and I went to visit
him. He was in an apartment, and he had filled the
refrigerator with food for us and had given up his room
and treated me like a queen. He was really a changed
man.

Recently, I received a call from my brother Harvey. He
said, "I just want you to know that all those times I was
mean to you when we were teenagers is because I was
trying to scare you because I didn't want you to follow in
my footsteps because you were beginning to go down
the wrong path as I had." As a teenager I hadn't
understood why he did those things. I always felt he
hated me. This phone call healed my heart, and I began
a deep weeping within me. Then, after he got saved, he
started bringing all his friends. He said, "You know,
Diane, when you're walking up these steps, it's as if
Jesus is walking up these steps." I knew it was the
presence of God. He said, "I've never met a holier
woman than you." I couldn't believe it! This was my

brother! He would bring his friends, and we'd pray for them and minister to them. Now my brother and I are very close.

My Siblings

I never learned about my father's family history; I can't go back any farther than dad except I heard that he was part Cherokee. I did know a few cousins and my half siblings and dad's youngest brother who we sometimes visited, while growing up, at his farm near Madera. In 2015 my husband and I went to visit him, Uncle Short, at an assisted care facility in Fresno, where at 94 yrs of age he was getting by. His mind was sharp, and he remembered in great detail the navy ship he served on in World War 2.

My husband shared with him about Christ but Uncle Short couldn't seem to go that direction and talked about other things. He told us then that he figured he might make it to 100 years of age. Two weeks later he was gone, a victim of the pneumonia he was just beginning to feel the day we visited him.

Many years before that, I went to a cousin's wedding in Madera, California. She was related to my dad. It was in the late 1990s and since my cousin was a cowgirl, I dressed all my 5 children in cowboy outfits.

While we were there, I took my children to the bathroom and a woman who I didn't know, who I found out was another cousin, began to prophesy to me. She said, "You're the chosen one. You're the one who will build the house of God." Then she looked at all the wedding guests, and said it again, aloud for everyone to hear. Then she said, "If anybody has money, give it to her." For a while, she would send us $100 a month. Before Uncle Short died he told me that that cousin had also died.

Then, I thought, somebody, somewhere, prayed for our family. I learned that my paternal grandmother was a praying, believing, woman, and I am sure that I received grace from God because of her prayers.

"He heals the brokenhearted. And binds up their wounds."

— Psalm 147:3 NASB

Chapter 5
My Aunt

When I was younger, I went to a summer program that helped teens who did not have fathers to get jobs.

I worked for the Salvation Army and at a swimming pool. So that's how we were able to buy our school clothes. I worked and went to school and had little time for much else. Then at 14, my mother took me to the priest to find out what was needed to become a nun.

Perhaps because of the conditions that I was under, I began to rebel. I started thinking that I wanted to go live with my aunt, who lived in Tucson, Arizona. When a child gets something in their head, they push for it. I definitely pushed and my mother just didn't know what else to do with me, so she said, "Okay, I'm sending you to Arizona."

My aunt was my mother's half-sister, and she cast spells and practiced witchcraft. When I went to live with her, she began to teach and train me in all her ways, to be a "spiritual" leader in the family. People would pay her to cast spells on their enemies. I stayed with her for about nine months, and then my mother allowed me to come back home.

You know, in Mexican culture, they have what they call white magic, where you dispel powers or spells that have been put against you. So, if someone threw a spell on someone, my mother would come to cleanse and break it. Mother did the white magic, and my aunt did the black magic. So, I came home to my mother's house. However, after those experiences with my aunt, I was just a mess as you can imagine. Yet, there was something in me, deep down, calling me and pulling me to God. I always said, "If there's a God, I want to know him."

When I came back, things didn't get much better. I started a party life. I had learned a little bit of that in Arizona, and I looked like I was 18, so I could go into the bars. I started the party life, and along with that, I started taking drugs that I said I would never take. I went down roads that I had promised myself I would never go down. I also began smoking, because my mother was a smoker. I would smoke, and then I would go to the Catholic Church, and I would confess my sins. I desperately wanted freedom but was looking in all the wrong places.

Chapter 6
My Life is Yours

Being raised Catholic, I would go to the priest and confess my sins. He told me to do a particular number of Hail Marys and Our Fathers, so I would repeat them, and then I would go back and do the same things I was doing before, the same sins. I had not found freedom or peace. I was powerless, and I was not free.

One night, when I was 16, a friend of mine invited me to a Christian church. I went to the service, and the pastor said, "Does anybody need prayer?" I went up to the altar, and the pastor said, "Say this prayer." I repeated the prayer and asked Jesus into my heart; I asked Him to wash my sins away. And then something happened. All at once, everyone started hugging me, and I felt different. I said, "Wow, I've never experienced this love!" I really loved it; I realized that, at that moment, the desires for the world were not even there anymore. God just took all the desires after I prayed at the altar. The longing to drink alcohol and do drugs was gone. Before I received

Christ, I didn't want to live. I would cut myself, take pills, or try to take my life. I was never successful - God had protected me. After I came to know him, that lifted as well.

My mother was not an affectionate person. I don't remember her ever saying to me, "I love you," or anything like that as a child. Her response to my decision was not surprising. When I went home, my mother discerned that something had happened to me. She said, "You cannot leave the Catholic Church, and if you do, you will go to hell." It was as if the demons and spirits knew what had happened to me. Spiritual warfare increased and doors and windows would shut by themselves, and I had a lot of demonic visitations. They didn't want to let go of me. At times, it was as if I could feel spirits flying around in the room.

I used to watch a lot of TV and scary movies before I knew Christ, but after I was saved, that was gone too. I said, "I don't want to watch that anymore, I don't want to watch scary movies," and I never did. I would just go to my room and read my Bible, and then I would go to any church I could find. I always felt peace at church. But when I came into my house, I would feel a demonic presence and was tormented. So, if my church didn't have a service, I was always looking for one that did.

My family never physically tried to stop me from going to church, but they would often say, "I think Diane has gone off her rocker. I think she needs to go to a mental institution." This was because I didn't want to go to parties. I didn't want to do what the world was doing anymore. So, at 16 years old, they told me I was crazy.

Even after I was saved, I still needed a lot of deliverance from spiritual bondage. The witchcraft that I had opened to had deep roots in my life, and I don't think the pastors where I attended church believed that a convert to Christ needed bad spirits to be driven out. I really didn't know what to do with my life anymore. I knew I didn't have what it took, academically. I told my mother, "Mom, I want to go to a Christian school, and I'm going to work to pay for it." She refused to let me go. So, then I thought, what am I going to do? My thoughts were so far beyond school. I didn't know what to do with my life.

My best friend, who brought me to the Lord, was a runaway. Her mother was Christian, but her stepfather was abusive. So, my mother took her in. My brother and she were boyfriend and girlfriend, and she lived with us. She would tell me, come on, Diane, let's go party, and she was the one that took me to church! I said, "Tammy, I'm tired of that. I'm done with that kind of life. I don't want it." Then, my brother, to get out of the gangs, joined the army. He needed to get out of Victorville; he needed a new life. He and Tammy married, and they had a child. They were living in El Paso, Texas, on the army base. Tammy asked me to come and stay with her because my brother would be gone all the time. I went to stay with her because I didn't know what else to do with my life. School wasn't anything I could succeed in, nor could I think of any career I could succeed in.

When I got to El Paso, the first thing I did was look through the Yellow Pages for a church. I found one and I started attending. My brother's friend, who was a Christian, would take me to church, and we started dating and got engaged.

I still thought, well, what am I going to do with my life? We began planning our lives together, where we were going to live, and when we would marry. We had purchased our engagement rings but something inside me was telling me that I needed to go visit my mom. I just had a feeling I needed to go see her. I took a bus back to Victorville and after arriving at my mother's house, I began hearing a voice inside me urging me not to marry that man.

I responded, "OK." So, I thought, what am I going to do now? How am I going to tell him? When he called and asked when I was coming back, I told him, "You know what? I don't want to hurt your feelings. I'm going to send these rings back to you because I don't want to marry you. I don't feel like I love you in that way." The young man got very, very angry and he started punching the walls. He was in the army, and I found out that he was abused as a child. I probably would have been a punching bag for him, but God is so good that He protected me from harm and heartache.

One day, a friend who was my next-door neighbor, came and said, "Why don't you go to beauty college?" I lied to the school and said that I had my high school diploma, and they enrolled me in their course. I was about eighteen years old by then and started drifting away from the things of God and could feel the demonic forces pulling me back to the world. I was really struggling. It was as if the spirit of rebellion was coming upon me again. I felt like I was trying to run away from the Lord. And I knew that I was in the wrong environment.

I was invited to a church where they were playing a movie about "The Rapture." A guy friend had taken me to church that day. During the movie I shouted out to him, "Get me out of here. Get me out of here." I felt like there was a war for my soul. So, he took me to a place in Victorville that was a viewpoint where you would look down and see the city. When he turned on the radio, someone was preaching. I responded, "Shut that off. Take me home right now!" He took me home.

Then, I heard the Lord say to me, "You come back to Me now with all your heart because if you don't, you will not live. The devil has a plan to take your life this week." The devil comes to steal, kill, and destroy, and he was definitely after me. That's when I completely surrendered myself to God and I said to Him, "Ok, my life is yours."

> "The thief comes only to steal and kill and
> destroy; I came so that they would have life,
> and have it abundantly."
>
> — John 10:10 NASB

After that, I met Jane and Ray Oliver.

Chapter 7
Jane and Ray

I met Jane and Ray at the church in Victorville that I was going to. They became my spiritual parents. I desperately needed guidance and mentoring; I needed somebody to pour into me and guard me, and God sent them to me. They were God's gift to me and to the divine purpose of God for me.

Ray Oliver and Diane

I got mixed up into Kenneth Copeland's teachings of claiming my blessings, but I was so bound by the past witchcraft that my mind was not free. I would just repeat what I heard in all his tapes. I got completely involved in that, trying my best to serve and walk with God with all that I knew.

Jane and Ray learned about a missionary training center called Sommer Haven Ranch located East of Palmdale that was situated on 10 acres out in the desert. They were involved in a food ministry at their church and began bringing lots of donated milk to the Sommer Haven ministry. In July 1981 they invited me to go with them in their big motor home to spend the weekend at the ministry center. That's when I first met Sister Agnes Numer, when I was just 19 years old. She would be the one to lead and guide me through the following years.

It was about an hour drive from Victorville to Sommer Haven Ranch, and as we turned down the long entrance driveway, up ahead of us I saw a man wearing white overalls carrying a bag of raisin bread. I suddenly heard the Lord's audible voice, "This is your husband." I really wasn't looking for one, and I just kind of brushed it aside. We came into the main house, and I was introduced to Sister Agnes Numer, the 65-year-old godly leader of the ministry, and to various others. I remember that when people asked me how I was, I would answer in parrot-like speech, repeating the Copeland teachings I had learned, "I'm blessed going in and I'm blessed going out." Mere words, no reality.

Later that night, as the regular residents washed dishes, I listened to one of my Copeland tapes. I decided to "Evangelize" Sister Agnes and began telling her how she needed to listen to the Copeland messages; "They'll set you free", I said. She patiently listened to me and then said, "Honey, why don't you get rid of that junk and let the

Holy Ghost work in you?" I was shocked at her bold words, but they had power, and I felt something break off that had bound me. The next day I threw all the cassettes away. It was Sunday and in the morning service people prayed for me, and I fell under the power of the Holy Spirit, lying prostrate on the floor. I think I was completely knocked out and in spiritual surgery lying on the floor for two or three hours. Sister Teresa, one of the leaders there spoke out loud and said, "Diane is hungry for the Lord." The presence of God touched me deeply with such peace. Afterward, Sister Agnes asked me, "Why don't you come here and learn to hear and live by the Holy Spirit?"

Sister Agnes said that I was the first person that she had ever asked to come to be trained, normally people asked her. Then she said to me, "Finish your schooling first." I never finished things, and I needed to finish. So, two months later I finished beauty school, packed my bags, and moved to Sommer Haven Ranch around October 1981.

Chapter 8

"You're Not Going Back"

I was living at Sommer Haven in late November 1981 when my brother Harvey called and said my family wanted me to come home for Thanksgiving. Inside I didn't feel good about it; it was as if I could feel witchcraft and mind control again. My brother came and picked me up. However, on the way back to Victorville, he said, "You're not going back there."

I began to feel heavy demonic powers, like something or someone wanted to take me over. They took me to his wife Tammy's house. All at once, I felt like I was losing my mind; I had to get out, I just had to get out. I felt like I couldn't hold on to my mind any longer, like the demonic was taking me over. That's when I escaped into an unoccupied room at Tammy's house and with my last bit of sanity, called Agnes, and cried for help.

She immediately sent a group of people to come and get me, but it was an hour's journey to Victorville, and my situation was dire. She then called Jane and Ray, who lived nearby and asked them to please rescue me from Tammy's house. They drove up to the house within minutes and I, now feeling like I was losing my mind, suddenly fled out of the house, not knowing what I was doing or where I was going.

As I ran out of the house I heard a call, "Diane! here, come here!" It was Ray and Jane who had just driven up. As soon as I saw their van, I ran out and jumped in, and they took off.

The team that Agnes sent for me picked me up at Jane and Ray's home and took me to a safe house in the mountains at 2am. I just wasn't in my right frame of mind, I felt like I wasn't there, like something was very wrong.

I felt a demonic presence trying to take over, pulling me back spiritually to where I had been before. Shortly after, my family even called the police saying that I was held captive by a cult, and the police came to check on me. At that time, I would sleep with Agnes, and she would pray for me throughout the night. She was a Godsend. When she'd go minister, she would have me right by her side. I would go with her and serve her in whatever she needed. At the same time, she would train me to see natural things, to learn to be trained to know God's ways in the natural things as well as the spiritual things.

I remember once that she asked me to wipe down a table ...I thought it was clean. Then she would say, "Over there, look right over there, it's dirty and needs cleaning." I learned so much of God's ways through Sister Agnes, and I assisted her by packing her suitcases, doing her hair, and just being there for her. Many times, when she would teach the word, I would just sit there and receive that impartation. I spent a lot of time with Agnes and helped her with everything. She taught me a lot, in areas that I couldn't see, but she saw.

Agnes imparted godly things to me and trained me so that God could use me all over the world. It's such a breath of fresh air honestly, but I had to be trained to be able to flow into everything. Before I came, I don't think I even really had a personality. I think I was just very oppressed and depressed. I didn't want to live. I just had no purpose, no reason to exist. I didn't know much because I didn't have any training or teaching. I never thought, "Oh, I'm going to go into ministry." But God Himself brought me into ministry and Sister Agnes took me and trained me for His kingdom's work.

I remember the day shortly after getting home from being "rescued" that we had a powerful service. We had been dancing and worshiping, and the presence of God filled us, and that's when the police came and wanted to see "Diane Watson." My family had sent them there saying I was kidnapped and being held against my will. So, Sister Agnes walked me out to them, and then we talked to the police. They said, "We don't see any chains on you."

My family thought I was in a cult. Then, the police said, "Well, if we have people that need help, we know where to bring them." It was a difficult situation; I couldn't really have a lot of contact with my family since I knew they felt the way they did. Even though our relationship was restored after a year, I had to completely sever ties at the time because they didn't understand where God was leading me.

That was one of the hardest things I did in my life, but at the time it was necessary.

Chapter 9
The Root Cellar

I had just come back to the training center after the difficult situation where my family did not want to allow me to return. I could feel a battle brewing inside of me; a lot of past things were trying to come back.

I was working in the root cellar with Teresa, another coworker in the ministry. There was only one way into the root cellar and one way out. After we worked for a while, Teresa asked me to put something on the shelves. For some reason, my mind was not there, and I would do the opposite. I turned and looked at her and all at once, I began to feel rebellious, like a witch. She said that when she looked at

The Root Cellar

me, I looked like a witch, something was manifesting in my eyes.

She calmly said, "Let's go see Agnes." So, we went up the root cellar stairs into the house and I stayed in the living room. Teresa told Agnes that something was wrong with me. When they came out of Agnes' room, I was looking up into the corner of the room, and I could see demonic things. They began to pray for me against this spirit, and then I heard them tell me, "Your will is involved."

Teresa said to me, "Diane your will is involved, either you rise up, take authority and get rid of this, or you choose to get out." In myself, I then determined to rise up in the Spirit against the demonic that was binding me, and I told the devil to get out of my life. The power of God hit me so strong, and deliverance came, total deliverance.

"12 Lord, thou wilt ordain peace for us: for thou also hast wrought all our works in us. 13 O Lord our God, other lords beside thee have had dominion over us: but by thee only will we make mention of thy name. 14 They are dead, they shall not live; they are deceased, they shall not rise: therefore hast thou visited and destroyed them, and made all their memory to perish."

— Isaiah 26:12-14 KJV

Chapter 10
A Breakthrough

Another time, Teresa came outside while I was counting boxes of bread that we would distribute to the needy. I didn't know how to multiply. I would count box by box, and there were many boxes, so it took me a long time. Remember, school was never easy for me. Teresa showed me to count: 1,2,3,4,5 boxes across and 1,2,3,4 boxes top to bottom. Then she encouraged me to multiply the 5 boxes times 4 and get 20, the correct number of boxes. She saw that I was really struggling with just counting one by one, and I didn't know how to use the Times Table. Then I got so excited; I felt God gave me the revelation. The revelation came and brought understanding, so much so that it became natural, and I could do it. It is amazing what God can do when we trust and submit to Him!

People have always said I had incredible common sense and the spirit of wisdom. This combination was greater than any mental block I may have had before. When the

Spirit of the Lord was upon me in wisdom and common sense, God just revealed himself to me. It is a wonderful way of life.

At Sommer Haven by the Root Cellar

"For in him we live, and move, and have our being..."

— Acts 17:28 KJV

Chapter 11
The Training

At Sommer Haven there were a lot of young people who received training. We were taught to yield, or submit, to what the Holy Spirit was teaching us, and to be faithful to God and His word. There would be times in the food ministry where the food would come in at one or two in the morning and we'd have to be up to receive it and put it away and then, after that, even wash the dishes. If we didn't get the dishes done before, we would be doing them afterwards.

You could choose to be the one to go to bed or you could be the one to be there and be faithful to finish the job. It wasn't to say that when you needed to rest you couldn't rest but there were times where you had to go the extra mile and let Jesus be your strength.

Jesus was there in times of spiritual experiences, but he was also there at the sink! His presence was all around us. I always wanted to be the first one doing the dishes because I wanted to be with the Father. It wasn't just in a devotional in the morning that I learned to find God; it was in submitting to be willing to be a servant.

Jesus said,

> "...If any man desire to be first, the same shall be last of all, and servant of all."

> — Mark 9:35 KJV

In the mentality of this world, we see it in such a different light. We see the servant as someone lower, especially in developing countries. In some countries, being a servant is considered something lowly.

That's what Jesus was. He was the servant of all. He worked on the wood that He created. He washed His disciples' feet, which was a form of humility. A key to success in the Kingdom of God is humility. Humility is the key to God's heart. He is near to those who are humble and contrite.

> "For this is what the high and exalted One Who lives forever, whose name is Holy, says: 'I dwell in a high and holy place, and also with the contrite and lowly of spirit in order to revive the spirit of the lowly and to revive the heart of the contrite.' "

> — Isaiah 57:15 NASB

Chapter 12

No Flesh Will Be Glorified

I remember sitting next to Agnes, I could just sit at her feet all day. Agnes was always moved by the Spirit of the Lord. When I first came, some nights I would stay with her, and she would pray through the night for me. Other trainees would be lined up all through the night just to talk with her. There were times when I was so bound, I couldn't even really express what was within me. I remember just crying and Agnes would pray for me, and it brought such relief even though I couldn't get everything out.

Eventually, I was finally able to open more and get everything out. I remember that she'd even fall asleep while I was talking and then she'd wake up and give me the answer I needed. Agnes had been trained by the Lord to live by the Spirit of Wisdom and the Spirit of Counsel.

I think what was imparted to me the most was the "Spirit of Wisdom," because the Bible talks about not "...seeing

out of our own eyes and hearing out of our own ears."
Seeing by His Spirit is what has affected my life the
most.

One thing that I learned from Agnes, was the importance
of death to self. No one will be glorified but Jesus! No
flesh will be glorified! Every day is about yielding and
dying, yielding and dying, and it's a process. Once we
stop yielding and we begin to live for self, we begin to
lose. We must be content in whatever state we are in,
instead of relying on ourselves.

The process is not always easy. It can be painful and
traumatic. It can be beautiful and joyful. If you can't walk
with Jesus in the hard times, then the beautiful times will
not seem as beautiful. If we submit to the Lord and allow
Him to rescue us, then He will rescue us. For example,
one of those traumatic things can be depression that
leads to suicide. People can't handle the gross darkness
and often think of ending their lives. But even though the
enemy tries to kill us through suicide, God can rescue
us, as He rescued me.

He takes our trials and turns them into triumphs. I heard
someone say once to an atheist, "I've come back to my
Christian roots. I deteriorated when I began to believe
your philosophy."

> What shall separate us from the love of Christ?
>   Shall tribulation, or distress, or persecution, or
>   famine Or nakedness, or peril, or sword?
>
> — Romans 8:35

Chapter 13
Cocopah

In early 1983 Sister Agnes
sent me to the East Cocopah
Indian Reservation in
Southern Arizona, outside of
Yuma, for about 6 months to
live with Joe and Melinda
Rodriquez. In the 18 months
since coming to Sommer
Haven, I had learned to be
faithful and sincere with
Agnes' instruction, and she
then entrusted me to go
represent Jesus among a

*My Husband, James
Profet*

different culture. The East reservation, where Joe and
Melinda lived, was very small with only two or three
dozen houses built by the government for the native
peoples. It consisted of only a couple of roads and was
situated in a rural desert place off the beaten trail. The
whole East reservation was, at most, a half mile long by a

quarter mile wide. Friends of Sister Agnes who had gone through that place in the 60s told us that back then there were only mud huts for homes. It seems that the federal government had overlooked these indigenous peoples for a long time but "Found" them in the 1970s and built them houses, roads, clinics and water systems. The desert temperatures there could top 117 degrees, so I had to adapt myself to work early before it got hot and take it easy later. I helped Joe and Melinda in their food ministry and in training them and we would go deliver donated food and pray for the Cocopah people near us and at the West reservation, about 10 miles away, and at the Cocopah reservation across the border in Mexico.

Joe and Melinda had come to know Sister Agnes and asked for her help reaching and evangelizing the native people. At that time, a lot of the older generation only spoke the Cocopah language whereas the younger generation spoke mostly English, so it made for an interesting situation. I remember Joe and Melinda's son, Joe Jr, only spoke English. His mother, Melinda, was bilingual, and Joe Jr's grandmother only spoke Cocopah.

Ministering among the Cocopah was challenging because it seemed very hard to break through cultural and spiritual barriers. Among the Cocopah youth, drugs, alcohol, paint sniffing, and vice dominated their lives. A lot of tragedy followed them. Some died in drunken accidents, some ended up in prison, some overdosed. One of them, Ralph, was brought by his mother to Sommer Haven in 1982 when he was 12 years old to be discipled in the Lord's ways. He was with us for most of a year but decided, against his mother's wishes, to return to the reservation. Sister Agnes was greatly grieved in the Holy Spirit with Ralph's decision because she knew that he wanted to follow the way of sin rather than of the Lord. Her words to our whole group the night before he left sticks to me to this day. "Ralph has decided to go back to the reservation", she paused and then continued, "And the hell he's going into is much hotter than the hell he came out of." We all shuddered. Sister Agnes was prophetic, and we knew that the Lord was speaking through her. Ralph went down the wrong path and ended up in an Arizona prison for about 20 years. He would call Sister Agnes by collect-call from prison every so often, and Agnes would have Jamie, my husband, pray for him. A short time after Ralph was released from prison he overdosed and died.

In those days, the Cocopah nation was called a dying nation due to so many young people on the reservation dying. I remember the Lord gave me the scripture about doing good works that they may see the Father and glorify Him.

> "Your light must shine before people in such a
> way that they may see your good works, and
> glorify your Father who is in heaven."
>
> — Matthew 5:16

I used to go clean the homes of the Cocopah— it was my way of showing them the love of the Father.

Joe and Melinda's son, Joe Jr, also known as Sonny, came to know the Lord through a revival. He received the Lord, and then we worked together with his family. Later, Sonny married, and he and his wife Melanie continued faithful in ministry. God's fruit continues even to this day. Sonny's life was transformed, and he made a deep commitment to the Lord. It was very beautiful to watch God change his life. Later, Sonny and Melanie went as missionaries to the Philippines for a year.

While Sonny was on the reservation, God gave him favor and the fruit of his life was evident. He also became a member of the tribal council. It was beautiful to see this, because so many of their youth died young. In ministry, you see those willing to yield their lives and who allow the Holy Spirit to work in them, but you also see many who do not yield and who lose the communion with God and drift back to the world. As a missionary I just learned to persevere in the name of the Lord trusting that He is always working and, in the fear of God, to watch over my own soul lest I should also fall away.

Chapter 14
Our Wedding

After months at Cocopah, the Lord prompted me to go live with my Mexican aunt and uncle across the border in San Luis, Mexico, and Agnes said she felt good about it, so I went. My aunt had a little house behind her house which wasn't finished but she rented it to us for 20 dollars a month. Agnes sent a crew of people to come and put in electricity and build a kitchen and make it livable for us.

Then, a young family we knew from Tijuana, Delia, Henry and little Henry, came to live with me. I was working with the youth there for several months. I saw a store one day on the way to take Henry to school, and the Lord said, "Go ask them for the food that they don't sell and give it to the needy." So, I asked the store owner, and they began to give us boxes of food. We did not have any money, yet they would give us food. We did not have a car so we would carry boxes of food on our heads. When we got home, we would sort the food and clean it and put it in bags.

The Spirit of the Lord began to move in that area where I lived, and young children would give their lives to Jesus. It was amazing. They were filled with the Holy Spirit and became my team. They would come, pick up the food, bag it, and we would all be praying in the Spirit. We would go house to house, give the food to the people and evangelize.

One day, I used someone's phone to call Sister Agnes, and she said, "I am sending you help." That help was Jamie. So, we began to do ministry together. One day Jamie said, "I think we need to pray." I said, "OK, what are we going to pray for?" Jamie said, "Against the spirit of marriage. I think people are putting us together just because we are single." I replied, "OK," and we prayed. We prayed and we rebuked the spirit of marriage. Then again, maybe two weeks later, Jamie was struggling again. I was very careful not to flirt with Jamie, but I knew what the Lord had told me that he was my husband. The Lord said to keep my eyes on Him, and that the person He had for me was doing the same. God also told me he would bring that one, in His time. So, my motivation wasn't for a husband; my motivation was for Jesus. I loved Him and served Him.

A few weeks later, the Lord said, "Tell Jamie what I told you." So, I told Jamie about what happened when I first saw him and what the Lord told me.

"The Lord told me too," Jamie said. He told me later that the Lord had whispered to him to give me a kiss, but he was way too scared to do it.

Jamie said, "Well let's pray together." We held hands and prayed, and the presence of God filled the room. It was as if we just wanted to be prostrate before Jesus. It was that type of holiness, so then we knew the Lord had joined us together.

We decided we had better cross the border and talk to Agnes who just happened to be close by ministering on the Cocopah reservation. My uncle who lived next door to my aunt had a truck. He had to cross the border over to Calexico, Arizona to pick cantaloupe and melons, so he gave us a ride to Joe and Melinda's house. We went into Agnes' room, and we told her we felt like it was God's will to be married. She just looked at us and said, "I don't know about this. I want to talk to Jamie by himself." When I walked out, I was overwhelmed. I thought, is this the enemy? I really doubted it because I thought the Lord would have already talked to Sister Agnes.

So, as I was walking out, Omer, Agnes' right hand in the ministry, who had been sleeping on the couch, came in and said to Agnes, "I don't know what is going on here, but when Jamie and Diane came this morning, I saw them as one."

Well, Omer confirmed it, and Agnes agreed that Jamie and I were going to get married.

We drove back home to Agnes' ministry center that night. Every time someone returned from another country, they would share during the nightly service. It was our time to share. Agnes was the only one who knew what was going on. Jamie played the guitar and while he was singing, he stood up in the middle of the song and said, "I have an announcement. Diane and I are getting married." I remember thinking how odd it felt. Everyone was shocked. Jamie and I were married in November 1983 after only a 3-week engagement.

Jamie's generosity was another thing that drew me to him. He had money in the bank, but everything changed when he came to Sommer Haven. He had such a burden for all the speakers that would come and do missionary work. He did whatever he could to help them out.

Our Wedding

He said he remembers when he took the last money out of his account. He was obedient as he listened to the Lord and took a big, deep breath, and said, "Okay, God, this is it!" He never felt any lack afterwards.

God blessed our wedding, and the Lord provided everything we needed.

Our wedding invitations said, "This is the day that the

Lord has made; we will rejoice as we come together as one, purposed for the Kingdom of God..."

A local pastor from the Nazarene Church let us use his church and fellowship hall for free. Someone else made and gave us our wedding cake, the food for the reception came from donations from our food ministry and special food items that normally did not come in came in at that time.

Diane and Jamie Profet with Rev. Agnes I Numer

Wedding Day with Parents

A precious sister even flew in from Texas and brought us our wedding rings as her gift.

And so, we were married, and Sister Agnes officiated our wedding. There were a lot of prophetic words. I wish I still had a recording of what was said. The day was such a blur, a mix of beautiful emotions. On our honeymoon we just wanted to go back to the mission field; we just wanted to minister to people. That was our life.

Two weeks later, after fixing up Jamie's old car we went back to our house in Mexico. Jamie said, "Well, we're not going to have children right now; we are living by faith." When anyone went out to minister, the Lord provided for them. Agnes always provided food and supplies, but we had to trust the Lord with everything else. We lived by faith. That's what she taught us to do.

When Jamie had said we're not going to have children soon, the Lord audibly spoke to me and said, "You will, and you will have them right away." When I told Jamie, what the Lord said, he said, "Well, whatever God wants." After three months, Jamie woke up and said, "Diane the Lord just told me you're pregnant and it's a boy." That week I got sick, I went to the doctor, and he told me I was pregnant.

When I came back, Jamie asked, "What are we going to name him?" At that time, I wasn't knowledgeable in the Bible, and I did not even know that there was an Isaac in the Bible, to be honest, and that name just blurted out of my mouth. I only knew of one person in school with that name. When I said, "Isaac," the presence of God filled the room, I was speaking prophetically, and the name Isaac just came out of my mouth. I was surprised because it didn't come from me; it came from the Holy Spirit.

After that I had four more children, and each child's name was a testimony that the Lord gave us. I never thought of the name. I never said I'm going to research a name. The Lord always gave us the name. He is so faithful.

Chapter 15
San Luis

Our time as a married couple in San Luis was short. We only had two months living there married and doing ministry to the community, when we foolishly became involved with a Mexican political conflict in February 1984. For a fleeting moment we seemed to be "Heroes" but nearly became "Zeroes." Jamie was raised in a household in which his father was involved in American politics, and he expected Mexico politics to be as nice as, seemingly, was American politics. Not so! The mayor of San Luis was a good man who we interacted with to help the community, and he supported what we did.

But he was from the PAN party, and the Governor of the state was from the PRI party and there's bad blood between them. Some conflict arose and the governor sent pickups with armed soldiers to San Luis as an intimidation tactic and thousands of citizens of San Luis, who loved their mayor, surrounded the city hall offices all night long where the mayor and his staff barricaded themselves, to protect them from the governor's hostility. Well, we showed up amid that tension saying that we wanted to speak to the mayor. His bodyguards escorted us into the inner chambers where the mayor and a slew of his staff awaited our words.

We were escorted in and received with honor as if we were the president. We told the mayor that God has placed him in that position, and the next morning's newspaper ran the headline "Fausto says "God put me in this office."" A little while later we were escorted out and drove to our little rented cottage in the town and noticed we were being followed.

At home, Jamie perceived some danger and wanted to drive across to Arizona, to Joe and Melinda's house. But I felt so tired I said, "No, you go, I'll stay here and sleep." Jamie said, essentially, "Not on your life! Get up! We're going to Joe's house and getting out of here." We crossed the border and upon arrival at Joe's house there was an urgent message to call home to Sommer Haven should they see or hear from us. When the phone call connected with Teresa, at Sommer Haven, she exclaimed,

"Jamie, thank God you called, where are you?"

"I'm at Joe's house"

"Thank God"

"Where is Diane?"

"She's here with me"

"Thank God! "DO NOT GO BACK TO MEXICO!! "Your lives are in great danger there, the Holy Spirt showed us that you and Diane would just disappear, never to be seen again. We have had heavy intercession for your lives for about 2 hours now."

Needless to say, we didn't return to our Mexico home that night but drove the 300 miles to Sommer Haven and remained there for a week. When it felt safe, we drove back to our little house in San Luis late at night just to grab our things and then left San Luis for good. We found out later that the day after we talked to the mayor and went over to Arizona, police cars were patrolling up and down the street and looking toward our house as if looking to see if our car was there.

Chapter 16
- James Profet's Testimony
By James Profet

My parents were devout Catholics at one point in their lives, but atheism crept in, and they just stopped going to church. I have no memory of them ever talking to me and my sisters about their decision to no longer go to church, but weekly church attendance was part of my cultural upbringing, so I continued attending every Sunday riding my bicycle the short seven-minute ride over and up the hill to the church.

At age 12, in the summer of 1969, as I neared the church, riding my bicycle up the hill, I was looking down on the ground as I leaned over the handlebars to get leverage to climb up the grade. Suddenly, I felt words forming inside of my chest. "Where in the world did that come from" I asked myself. Words had formed inside of me, yet it was not OF me, its origin was not my own mind. In me, but not of me, this I knew for sure. And then I listened to the words. Two words; "Look Up!" I lifted my head and saw a car coming down the hill right toward me. I quickly veered aside and as the car passed exactly where I had been riding, just a mere few feet from me now, I saw that there was no driver! Someone parked at the top of the hill and didn't apply their parking brake and when they went into the church the car began rolling down the hill silently, right toward me. My mother said to me later that the guardian angels must have been watching over me.

Five years passed and, in the summer of 1974, I was a 17-year-old high school graduate with a summer job parking cars at a restaurant situated right on the beach in a Southern California beach town. One evening a Christian evangelist who was testifying about Christ to the many lost souls along the beach also found me in my parking lot. He testified to me and in the conversation said "Jamie, someday you'll stand before God on the day of judgement, where will you end up?" A most unpleasant topic. During the conversation a sudden sense and awareness came upon me of the presence of an invisible, powerful, large and intelligent being and it was standing immediately behind the evangelist. I don't know how I knew, I just knew that this being was real and it was there, and I felt fear.

The next sense I had was that this being desired to lay hold of me and pull me close to itself as a friend. Though powerful, its desire was for my friendship, my fellowship, and somehow, I knew it was joined to the evangelist, almost as if assigned. I didn't tell the evangelist what I sensed, and he seemed quite oblivious to the being that was with him, but after that I ran away, the demons in me not letting my soul reach out to Christ.

A month or two later I began college at a small school in rural northern California. One of my roommates was a full-blown hippie from Ohio with scruffy beard and hair down to his backside whose vocabulary consisted of "Cool man, Groovy" and a few other choice San Francisco words. Three weeks later the hippie came into the apartment clean shaven, with short hair and a peaceful smile. "What happened to you, Brooks?" I exclaimed. "I found Jesus" was the reply. Well, that set up the whole rest of the school year for debates and challenges on my part to this man's belief. The demons of antichrist in me just had to prevail against his Christian faith. It didn't work. At school's end we turned our apartment in, said polite goodbyes and parted ways, me to LA, him to Ohio, surely to never talk again.

Two months later an ex-girlfriend from college invited me to her home for a party. She humiliated me quite badly in front of her friends and the next 5 days were pure hell for me of depression and suicidal thoughts. At my parent's home, in desperation and tears, I hid myself in the bathroom not wanting my sisters to see me cry and I blurted out something I had never uttered — "Oh God, please help me!" Immediately, within 2 seconds, all the oppression, depression and desperation came out of me, starting from my feet and coming out the top of my head. I was overjoyed! I looked at myself in the mirror, wiped away my tears, smiled at my image and went out, free from the darkness. Did I give God glory for the miracle He had just performed? Of course not, I was still full of myself — the gods of our own making don't surrender easily.

Fast forward 3 years and I'm 21 years old and lost spiritually and practically – no job, no career, no direction. My arrogance, antichrist mindset, pride, foul mouth, selfishness only worsened. I was living in Northern California but due to my nastiness, my girlfriend, Julie, who I'd had for a year, decided to leave me, and I took off back to my parent's home in Southern California. The next month, in June,1978 I received a phone call from Julie's brother, and he told me that Julie had died instantly in a head on crash with a drunk driver. The bottom fell out of my life and the wind came out of my sails. I was devastated. I caught the first plane back to Northern California to piece together what had happened in the accident and go to the funeral. I cried like a baby seeing Julie in a casket and I was the last person to leave her burial. She had taught me a little bit about God and asked me one day if I ever just talked to God because I had been raised Catholic and talking directly to God wasn't in my knowledge.

A few days after her funeral, back at my parent's home in Southern California, I passed a bookcase, and my eye caught sight of a Bible on the shelf. I froze and stared at the black book and then there came a voice inside my chest that spoke to me with a tone of firmness and authority that I remember to this day – "Pick up that book and READ IT!" I reached out to that Bible that I had never seen on that shelf and that I had never seen being read by anyone in my family and I began to read.

For the next several days I took time each afternoon to read the only thing I remembered from Catholic church – the Gospels: Matthew, Mark, Luke and John. Over those days, as I read, I felt drawn to the words of Christ, to the stories and the miracles and the purity of His teaching. And then the memory of 4 years prior came rushing back into my mind – the evangelist who testified to me in the restaurant parking lot. I tried to shake his memory, but I couldn't, all day long he was on my mind, and I decided I needed to find him. I obtained a number for him and called, and I told him who I was and that 4 years prior he had talked to me about Christ at that restaurant parking lot and he said he remembered me and asked what he could do for me. I answered, "I want to find out what all this Jesus stuff is about about." He invited me to an informal prayer gathering that evening and I made the step into the unknown – of calling out to a God I could neither see nor touch. I resolved it in my heart to reach out to Christ and to ask Him for forgiveness because I figured that maybe, just maybe, this man Jesus really was who He said He was – The Son of the Living God – and I also figured that if He really _was_, then He really _is_.

That evening, July 10,1978, I stepped out of the darkness and into the first rays of Living Light. Immediately some things radically changed in my life. No more blasphemous words nor angry tirades against incompetent drivers; peace had begun to settle into my heart.

And then the following month I remembered Brooks, my formerly hippie roommate. I dialed the Ohio phone information operator, and they gave me Brooks' number. I dialed him and he picked up the phone and I said "Brooks?" "Yes, speaking." "Brooks, this is Jamie Profet." There was a long silence and then a surprised response, "JAMIE PROFET!?!?" "Yes Brooks, how have you been?" I asked. "The Lord has been so good to me" he said. And then I responded with an overwhelming "WELL PRAISE THE LORD!!!" There was a stunned silence and then an incredulous "JAMIE, ARE YOU SAVED??!!" That was 47 years ago, and we still communicate. I've never forgotten what Brooks shared with me in that phone call. He told me that he had prayed for me all through that school year but that after we parted ways at school year's end, he told the Lord that Jamie was so impossible, so arrogant, so nasty, so self-willed that "God, not even you could save this boy." I think God took that up as a challenge.

I am so grateful for salvation. I am so grateful to the people who prayed for me. I am so grateful to Jesus and to my Heavenly Father that mercy was shown to me and such abundant forgiveness and kindness and grace was poured out upon me. I am a debtor to God, to give Him my life in response for the immeasurable goodness he has given to me.

Chapter 17

- The Father's Heart

By James Profet

The year following my conversion brought a big change
to my life. I was hired by a large Aerospace company in
September 1979 as an engineer's assistant and moved
out of my parents' house (for the last time) and was back
on my own living with 2 roommates in a rented
apartment. The workplace was a 3,000-employee high
tech company that designed and built navigation units
for cruise missiles, military aircraft, commercial jetliners
and others.

Among the employees were El Salvadorian refugees who
worked for a cleaning contract company whose main job
it was to sweep floors and empty trash cans in the many
hundreds of offices located throughout the facility. In my
time at that company, I never once ever witnessed one
of the regular employees ever acknowledge these
foreign, Hispanic workers or greet or thank or smile at
them. Even amongst my own immediate co-workers I
never saw them acknowledge or thank the cleaning

people for what they did. I couldn't understand the callousness and indifference of the regular employees toward the cleaning people, so I made a point to go out of my way to be friendly and kind whenever I saw them. I spoke very little Spanish in those days but with the little I knew I used it to converse with these refugees and talk about God and to just be a friend to them.

One day, in July 1980, the indigenous refugee woman whose job it was to sweep through my office area, came into my office pushing her broom and then stopped and began weeping and I asked her, in my limited Spanish, what was the matter? She explained that she was so sad because she was so lonely and that she was in this country with no family and no friends and with the civil war raging in El Salvador she didn't even know if her family there were dead or alive. She continued then to weep, and I didn't know what I should do. Unknown to my co-workers, was the presence of this young lady in my office cubicle crying and weeping with a desperate heart. I then stood up from my desk and did the only thing I could think to do - I placed my hand on the woman's head and prayed for her that God would grant deliverance and peace. When I finished, the young lady looked up at me with big brown eyes and wiped away her tears and smiled at me and said, "Ya me siento mejor, muchas gracias" Translated: "Now I feel better, thank you very much". At that she turned and left.

I remained standing in my office and pondering what had just happened. Then, suddenly, awesomely, I felt a heavy, holy, presence descending into my office. I was in the presence of the Holy, and I don't know how I knew, but I knew that it was the presence of the Father of glory. And then I heard His words inside my mind as He called me by my name. "Jamie, this is what is important to ME, this is what I care about". I understood what he meant. It was the simple showing of compassion and kindness and care to the young woman who had nobody else to turn to.

The woman was a person without physical beauty, education, refinement, wealth, resources, talent; all the things the world finds attractive and thus nobody cared about her but God cared about her and He showed me His heart and how He desires people to be compassionate and caring and helpful and willing to be a friend to those who haven't one. The Father continued, and I saw him point out all the high-tech industry, the big financial institutions around about the area and He said, "And all the rest of this is only a means unto an end." And then, referring back to helping the woman, "But this is what is important to ME". The voice then stopped and slowly the very heavy presence began to lift from my office. I remained standing and wept uncontrollably for a long time.

Six months later I resigned from my job and went to live at Sister Agnes Numer's Sommer Haven Ranch, a missionary ministry, to be trained as a missionary. Six months after that I met my future wife, Diane, who also later came to live at the same ministry to be a missionary.

Chapter 18
- The Prophecy
By James Profet

In January 1982, after being at Sommer Haven for about a year, Sister Agnes accepted an invitation for us trainees, the "kids" of Sommer Haven Ranch, to attend a special service in Los Angeles conducted by a brother, John Bishop, who led a ministry of prayer for the nations. Diane had recently come to Sommer Haven and about 40 of us drove down from Palmdale to the Los Angeles meeting.

The meeting hall was filled with round tables and chairs and we all sat wherever we wanted to. I remember nothing of the service but after preaching the minister asked for all the attendees to come to the front and form a single line, shoulder to shoulder to receive personal prayer. Upon moving to the front, navigating around the round tables, by sheer "coincidence" Diane and I found ourselves next to one another in the prayer line, shoulder to shoulder, she on my right.

The minister was in front and down a way to the right of us and he decided to begin praying for people at the other end of the line, to our left. As he passed directly in front of us while walking to the end of the line, he suddenly jerked hard as if hit by divine anointing. He immediately turned around and faced me and Diane.

As I looked into his blue eyes something happened to me that I have never again experienced. His blue eyes suddenly became portals of the Infinite One and it was as if I was looking through his eyes into eternity. The minister's eyes welled up with tears that flowed down his cheeks, and he looked at me and then Diane and reached out a hand to take my hand and he reached out his other hand to take Diane's hand. He then prophesied to us and said, "God is going to use you two with such love...." He said more but by that time my mind was racing with shock and carnal thoughts that said, "Oh no, this man thinks we're married!"

I heard nothing else that he said and when it was time to sit down both Diane and I quickly left in opposite directions and said nothing to each other.

I was absolutely embarrassed by what had transpired, and yet, I pondered it in my heart.

Chapter 19
A Pair of Shoes

A special incident comes to mind that happened in 1993. While at Sommer Haven, before we moved back to Mexicali, Mexico in September, we were asked to share testimony, preach and pray for people in North Hollywood at a Full Gospel Businessmen's breakfast meeting. We were in a hurry to get to the early morning meeting, which was over an hour away, and I quickly grabbed my shoes and jumped into the car.

When we arrived at the venue, we got out of the car and my husband wiped the dust off his shoes because it was very dusty where we lived. I looked at my shoes and realized I had one high heel shoe and one low heel shoe that were also totally different shoes and of completely different colors.

And I said to my husband, honey, do you have any money? I can't go in like this. Jamie laughed at my shoes. It was early in the morning, and every store was closed, but we saw a thrift store and people were waiting in line for it to open. My shoes were very noticeable, so I shared with the other people what had happened and why I was in line at the thrift store to find a pair of shoes.

When the doors finally opened, I could not find one pair of shoes that fit me. We missed the breakfast part of the event after which we were supposed to speak. We had to get going because time was running out. A woman who had been listening to my story and watching me the whole time approached me said, "What size are you?" I said, "I'm a nine." She said, "The other day I was in a store and the Lord prompted me to buy these shoes, you can have them, I'm not even this size of shoe." They were the exact size, and they fit my outfit just like they were tailored for it!

This is how the Lord worked and showed me how caring and loving He is to those who follow Him and love Him with their whole heart.

Chapter 20
Quechan and Mexico

For about 8 months in 1984-1985, we lived on the Quechan Indian Reservation, located in far Southeast California, a stone's throw from Yuma, Arizona. The Lord had worked through Sister Pat Capwell from Sommer Haven to open a door at the reservation and God's life was with us as we ministered to the local people. We lived at the Yuma Methodist Indian Mission complex, on the reservation, with Gabriel and Laura, another couple from Sommer Haven, and a couple of native women who oversaw the mission. We worked as a team and began a food ministry and reached out to the local community. Life flowed to the tribal people and some were mightily touched. Our first child, Isaac, was born while we lived there.

Jamie had learned a lot about mechanics, electrical and refrigeration while at Sommer Haven and he had a burden to set up a walk-in refrigeration unit at the mission to preserve food. It was amazing how it all worked out and he sought donations of materials from various companies around the area. A long story short, Jamie prepared the ground, had 3 truckloads of concrete poured, received a truckload of used donated refrigeration equipment from Los Angeles, assembled the prefabricated panels, ran electrical, set up compressors, ran tubing and completed a 12 foot by 48-foot walk-in refrigeration unit with 3 cold rooms, up and running with only about $250. He built a 20 ft by 52 ft roof on top of the cooler unit and a raised platform to offload food boxes onto. We were able to store fresh food supplies that we then gave out to the community. The food ministry was beautiful in that it brought people together for a common and godly purpose and it brought life to all who helped work in it.

 It was an ambitious project, but it had a short life. In April 1985 Agnes called us back to Sommer Haven and sometime after that Gabriel and Laura were called to the Blackfeet reservation in Montana. We returned to Quechan later in 1985 for a little while because I gave birth to my 2nd son, Benjamin, near the mission, but from the beginning of 1986 only the local Quechan people were left to run the ministry. Jamie spent most of 1986 onboard the Spirit ship in Seattle and I joined him there in early May. The cooler units ran automatically but still required maintenance and there was nobody who knew how to do it. In the summer of 1987, a rift developed between the people at the Yuma Methodist mission involved with the food ministry and in a heated, abrupt decision, the mission's board decided to shut down the food ministry and have the coolers dismantled. Within a couple weeks Jamie disassembled and moved everything away. Sadly, as the equipment left, so also did the life of God. The ministry at the mission faltered and the visitation of God left that place. I'm sure that souls were lost.

In early 1984 an open door came to us to meet people in El Centro, CA and a connection to meet Christians in Mexicali. We ended up staying in the home of a couple there and became acquainted with members of a large church. We felt to return to Mexicali in early 1985 and promoted the Isaiah 58 vision among the Christians and churches there. One incident that showed us again the hand of God to protect us occurred in February 1985. We had borrowed a large diesel bobtail truck from a man in Mexicali and went with a team of volunteers to El Centro to pick donated vegetables for distribution among the poor in a new residential colony on the outskirts of Mexicali. All the "Houses" then in that area were made of cardboard and plastic and we wanted to bring donated food for the people.

To cross the truck with its full load of harvested vegetables, Jamie obtained a letter from the head Mexican border official asking the on-duty personnel to grant us entrance to Mexico. But something went wrong and Jamie, after entering Mexicali, was being followed by 4 undercover state police agents in a car who tried to force him to stop.

I was following Jamie in our car and was unaware of what was going on. But this car of state police was trying to force Jamie, in the big diesel truck, to stop on the side of the road. By an amazing circumstance, due to construction on the road, the car with the agents was forced to proceed ahead past a stop light, and Jamie, instead of continuing straight, to where the police were waiting for him, made a quick left and zigzagged around the city streets to lose them. The next morning, we proceeded with our plan and freely distributed the vegetables in the poor colony. Shortly afterward we left Mexicali and went back to Quechan and then back to Sommer Haven.

> "The one who loves his life loses it, and the one who hates his life in this world will keep it to eternal life."
>
> — John 12:25

In September 1993 we returned to Mexicali to minister among the poor colonies. We had 5 children then and lived in a donated school bus that was converted into a motor home. We had been granted permission by a property owner to park and operate out of his large 1-acre property on the southern outskirts of Mexicali. The property had a ball court and patios and other amenities that made it excellent for hosting children. We quickly set up to host children every Saturday for 4 hours that included Bible lessons, crafts, sports and lunch. It was a blessed time. As well, we reached out into other poor communities to bring food and other supplies, and Jamie would play his guitar and sing gospel songs and minister to the people. We met a woman there named Natalia who became a disciple of ours and she helped us extensively in the outreach to the communities. She came to Christ through our ministry and was a beautiful addition to our team.

We heard about the nearby brickyards with people who made bricks by mixing mud with their feet. The children there hadn't ever been to school and Natalia and I used to go there to teach classes, using a chalkboard to instruct the children in Spanish. In addition to school lessons, we also taught them about the Bible. We also continued every Saturday ministering to the children from the community, and I would cook for them – and around 70 children came each week. We held vacation Bible school and ministered to them regularly. Many of the children gave their lives to the Lord.

When the mothers saw me cooking for their children, they said, "We want to come and help." They got saved as well and became my helpers. My own children would help with the ministry and take responsibility to help the other children. We had many helpers who loved the Lord, and we did this for many months.

There were times in Mexico that we didn't have money for gas to get around. Amazingly, sometimes the poor and oldest ladies would give us pesos to sustain us. During that time, there was a woman who had cancer. I said, "We must get medicine for this woman." We all got our money together, and I heard,

> "He who has pity on the poor lends to the Lord,
> And He will pay back what he has given."
>
> — Proverbs 19:17 NKJV

Right after that, we received an unexpected check for $350 that came from friends in Canada.

There was another woman who lived in the streets. She had a lot of children and was out of her mind and very unkept. She would come and just sit where our ministry was, and God began to change her life. She began to brush her hair and take care of her children. Her husband, who was an alcoholic, got saved as well. It was just beautiful. There was a wonderful presence of God moving among the children and the families.

Then in April 1994, problems arose with the landowner where we lived, and after prayer, we heard in the Spirit to move away. A door opened for us to check out a house with an attached chapel that had been offered to Sommer Haven missionaries in a small village just outside of Vicente Guerrero, about 4 hours south of Tijuana along the West coast of Baja California. The Mexican American couple who had the house asked us to come and live there and be the pastors so they could move to their trailer about 2 miles away on a large property they were developing for horses and farming. The village had no electricity, no running water, and no phone. Jamie and I and another Sommer Haven missionary drove the 9 hours from Sommer Haven to check out the property. Afterwards, as we started the long journey home, Jamie asked me what I thought about coming there to live. I felt excited about it and told my heart to Jamie. He however was very negative and said, "There is nothing in my heart to come here at all." Within a minute or so Jamie then said, "I heard the Spirit say to me, "Come, it is for your preparation.""

We lived there for about 18 months. We learned to adapt and use a solar panel and battery in our motor home and kerosene lamps in the house for light. We also used a generator to run lights in the chapel for night services. Our refrigerators burned propane for power to stay cold, and we could refill the small propane tanks at a local supplier. We hauled water in a big plastic tank with a pickup truck and used the generator to power a pump that pumped water into a tall concrete tank that provided gravity pressure water for the sink and shower and toilet. It was primitive living, especially with 5 small children.

There were only two buildings on the side of the village where we lived, and the rest of the homes were made of cardboard and plastic. We did the same thing in that village as we had done in Mexicali and Natalia came to help us. Every Saturday we hosted the local children for several hours, fed them, taught them and ministered to them. We had church services twice a week in the warm months, on Sunday morning and Wednesday evening, but in the winter, nobody came to the evening service. The villagers lived a primitive life with no heating and no electricity, and in the cold, dark winter, the whole village was in bed by 6 pm. We visited homes and gave donations of food to the villagers and prayed with whoever wanted it.

It was a different experience for us, and it seemed like the Lord was teaching us to rest in Him. We had become so accustomed to continual work for 15 years and now it seemed like we had to learn to slow down and abide in the Lord. It was hard for Jamie, but he was learning to be still and rest in God and be delivered from having to always be busy.

MEXICO

MEXICO

MEXICO

MEXICO

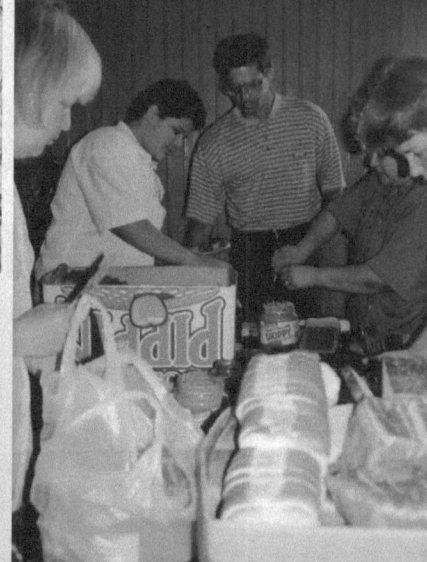

Chapter 21

- Chinese Refugees in Mexico

By James Profet

In May 1993, a situation and series of events unfolded upon us that ended up having unexpected twists and turns that make this story worth telling and remembering.

Sister Agnes received an unexpected visit from a Mexican woman we didn't know, who asked for help with food and supplies for an urgent need in Mexicali. A ship had arrived at the port of Ensenada, Baja California, carrying its regular cargo along with approximately 300 undocumented refugees from China. Their intention was to remain hidden and travel north to enter the United States illegally. However, it is quite hard to keep 300 Chinese people hidden in a town of Mexicans for more than a short time and their presence became known and they were all detained by Mexican authorities.

So, where do you place 300 Chinese people? The Chinese refugees were taken to the only available facility in the region large enough to accommodate them—the sports arena in Mexicali. There wasn't enough food, showers, toilet paper, or clean, working toilets for all the people detained there.

The Mexican woman, Rosa, who first came to talk with Agnes, knew that the Chinese would need food and supplies, so we loaded her van with food. Jamie and I, and a few others packed personal things and drove in a separate vehicle with Rosa the 5 hours down to Mexicali. Rosa was well known in the region as a humanitarian, and through her, we were able to access the sports arena to prepare and serve food to those detained there. One of the Chinese men spoke some English, and we talked with him while making food and got to know him. They were kept in the sports arena while the Mexican government negotiated with the Chinese government over how to repatriate these refugees.

After a day of feeding 300 people, we crossed the border to Calexico and had a bite to eat at McDonald's. We paused to give thanks for our food.

A man approached us and said, "I noticed you saying grace before eating, you must know the Lord". We conversed a while and then he told us that he was the chaplain of the federal detention center in El Centro, and he was trying to get Chinese Bibles over to the Sports Arena but couldn't get in. We told him that we could help, he gave the Bibles to us, and we brought them the next time we gave food.

It took a considerable amount of time for the two governments to negotiate. During that period, we continued offering support—providing food, praying with them, and helping in any way we could. We then returned to Sommer Haven to load a large truck with fresh supplies. After the drive back to Mexicali, we unloaded everything at the sports arena.

However, before I left Sommer Haven to drive to Mexicali, Teresa approached me and presented me with a few photos she had taken with us and with Mexican authorities who were supervising the refugees. Teresa told me that she really felt she was supposed to give me the photos to take back with me to Mexicali. The following morning when we arrived back at the sports arena, it was empty. We were told that the negotiations had been completed, and all 300 refugees had been taken from the sports arena to the Mexicali airport the night before.

We went to the Mexicali airport which is only 2 or 3 miles south of the US border. It is in the open desert with only sand between the airport and the border. There was a DC-10 aircraft parked with engines idling.

Well, unknown to us, until we arrived at the airport, some of the Chinese refugees, overpowered their guards and made a break towards the US border.

The guards were eventually able to restrain about half of them but that means that well over a hundred Chinese escaped into the night. Most of the escapees went North to the US border and were apprehended by US Immigration and placed in detention.

We could feel the intensity of heavy oppression; we could feel the seriousness and the heaviness, and we wanted to get out of there fast. Even Sister Rosa who had clout among the big shots said to me, I think we better get out of here and fast.

Guards started pointing to us and murmuring, "It's your fault!". I had already seen that a Mexican police official had purposely trapped our car in the compound – we couldn't leave! I had never been so tempted in my life to run, and I was looking north towards the US border that now looked so inviting!

Thank God for Sister Rosa, she came up with a good plan, and said, "I think we just need to start making sandwiches". And we did. Sandwiches flew out of our ice chest! We just happened to have the makings for lots of sandwiches with us. So, we made and served sandwiches and did so with big smiles on our faces even though we were shaking inside and wanted nothing more than to be on the north side of the border, in good ol' USA.

Finally, the big DC-10 aircraft with 170 or so Chinese on board took off. At that point, the officers and guards began leaving, and that's when we saw HIM, the head Mexican man overseeing the Chinese in the sports arena. He had been so friendly to us at the arena, but now, it's like he doesn't even know us. The tension in the air was palpable, and the heaviness could be cut with a knife.

Our car was trapped so we couldn't leave, and it was as if we were the ones to blame for 130 Chinese escaping.

That head officer in front of us had a loaded clip with bullets in his shirt pocket and he looked at me like I was the criminal responsible for this mess.

Then I remembered the photos given to him by Teresa. I pulled them out and showed the man, and the man was in some of them. And then, suddenly, the atmosphere changed, that head official smiled, took the photos, looked at them, and showed them to others who were around. They realized we were not to blame.

There was one photo with me and Diane and him and in the photo, we were smiling together. And then the man smiled, and it was all over. Other officials and guards came around and then they smiled and joked around, and it was over. Peace.

The policeman who blocked our car moved out of the way to let us leave. We said farewell, drove away, and thanked God for deliverance! We were so relieved, safe now, time to go home. We drove to Joe & Melinda's house in Arizona, finally safe, to spend the night there before leaving for Sommer Haven in the morning.

We went to sleep, but we were rudely awakened by Joe's phone ringing at about one in the morning. Joe answered it and said, "Jamie, it's for you". Jamie answered and it was Teresa, our friend from Mexicali, the aunt of the woman who spoke some English who helped us feed the Chinese. "Jamie, what are we going to do?" Half a dozen Chinese just showed up at my niece's house in the middle of the night". Well, while most of the Chinese, after the breakout, headed north towards the

US border, a few got disorientated and went south, including the English-speaking Chinese man, who had the phone number of one our friends, and a half dozen with him.

A Mexican man found this group of Chinese men walking down the road and gave them a ride. The English speaker then showed him the phone number, and the man called our friend. Our friend, Marta, told the man to bring the Chinese boys to her house, which he did, and it was still night. Marta housed them in an extra room she had.

The last place I wanted to go right then was back to Mexico but there was no choice now. In the morning Joe and I gathered food and drove to Mexicali, to Marta's house and met with the Chinese. Marta had a vision in which the Lord gave her a scripture about helping the foreigner, so Marta knew that this is what she was supposed to do. I told Diane that I was much more hesitant because of the day before. But we prayed and preached to the Chinese, and it had a good ending.

The English-speaking Chinese man had a wealthy uncle in New York and was able to get in touch with him. The uncle sent for all the Chinese men several days later and was able to get across the border and to New York. The English-speaking Chinese man stayed in touch with Marta for years afterward, having given his life to Christ and was doing well in New York.

As for the Chinese apprehended by the US Immigration at the border, they were taken to the federal detention center near El Centro and were there for a long time. The chaplain of the detention center who we had met at McDonald's days earlier, got Chinese materials for them and shortly afterwards, we met a Chinese man at a church who took interest in the refugees, and I brought him to El Centro to preach to the incarcerated Chinese there. Our Chinese friend continued going to El Centro occasionally to visit and disciple the inmates.

What an experience.

1985

SPIRIT SHIP
DON & SONDRA TIPTON
FOUNDERS
FRIENDSHIPS.ORG

Chapter 22

- Spirit Ship

By James Profet

In early October 1985, a small crew from Sommer Haven Ranch traveled to Tacoma, Washington to begin restoration of the MV Palisana, a 340-foot WW2 cargo ship that had been idle and unused since about 1957.

Don Tipton was the son of a friend of Sister Agnes Numer, and as I recall, Agnes had prophesied to Don that he would have ships to bring cargo, relief, and missionaries to poor areas along the ocean's edge. Don acquired the Palisana as a donation to his non-profit organization and took possession of the ship a few days before the crew arrived to begin restoration.

Imagine a small group of zealous but ignorant "missionaries" trying to restore an immense cargo vessel for travel across oceans. The first several months were only bare survival. The ship was essentially dead with no systems having been operated for nearly 30 years. There was no electricity, no heat, no water, no hot water, nor did any of the small crew have any knowledge of ships; there was nothing but persevering faith to help them. That first team was hearty and was eventually able to activate the ship's emergency generator for electricity and began making progress. The project was an amazing example of God's provision, as many groups of volunteers came and offered their help to the project.

The ship was moved in 1985 by the gracious donation of a Seattle area tugboat company to Bainbridge Island, at the Western edge of Puget Sound opposite Seattle. The Palisana was renamed "Spirit", and her new home was offshore about 100 yards from a boat repair company. There was no shore electricity, but at least a water hose and telephone line were run underwater and up to the ship to help the crew survive a little better. The emergency generator, though problematic, provided enough electricity for lights, galley stoves, air compressors, etc.

Agnes sent me to help with ship restoration in early February 1986. A whole book could be written about the Spirit Ship and its 5-year restoration and about the myriads of volunteers who helped restore her and Spirit's subsequent travels to Eastern Europe, West Africa and Central America, but that book has to be written by others more acquainted with the whole story.

I spent one year on board Spirit helping to restore the main engine and various other systems. When it became clear that my original plan to volunteer on board the Spirit for only two weeks would be extended indefinitely, Diane joined me in May 1986 to live on board with our two very young children, Isaac and Benjamin. Diane helped by teaching and caring for other volunteers' children, along with handling various other tasks, while I worked on the machinery and ship's systems.

In September 1986, Spirit Ship was again moved by tugboat to the Seattle waterfront where we could finally connect to shore power electricity. After making the connection to shore electricity, I shut down the emergency generator on board Spirit. I found out later that there wasn't even enough diesel fuel left for the generator to start again – **we had used the very last of our diesel fuel running the generator up to the very moment we no longer needed it!**

One incident I remember shows God's great providence in watching over us. We had to be extremely careful about our little son Isaac, who was just 2 years old but was as slick as a lick in escaping and running up on deck. The ship was docked out in the harbor and the main deck was at least 20 or more feet above the water. One day, Diane suddenly had a warning in her spirit, "Go find Isaac now, he's up on the deck". She rushed up just in time to see another crew mate grab hold of Isaac as he was about to step off the ship into the cold sea water below.

In early 1987, we returned to Sommer Haven Ranch.

FAMILY

Chapter 23
My Family

When the Lord spoke to me about my husband, Jamie, I was attracted to the love that he had for God. He had such a purity of love, and he would just sit and play his guitar. That's what drew me to him, the love that he had for Jesus. Even though we're very different, very, very different, it's the love of God that keeps us.

Isaac, my oldest son, was prophetic, sometimes he would give us advice. He would see things and have visions in the spirit, and what he saw would come to pass. His grandfather thought that it was his imagination, but we knew better.

Benjamin was my second eldest child; he was born on my birthday. He was very good with his hands. Benjamin could make something beautiful out of a bone.

Rachel, my middle child, had to deal with being the only girl among all her brothers. Rachel really wanted a baby sister, but that didn't happen. She was a busy bee; she liked to touch everything. There were also times when she would really rise up in the spirit and pray.

Our Family with all of my children

About the time my son Michael was born in 1988, Jamie was working on unloading 3 boxcars filled with 7,200 fifty-pound bags of wheat that had been donated for the Philippines. They had to unload all those bags by hand into trucks and then store them at the Los Angeles harbor. The Lord spoke to Jamie before Michael was born. Jamie wanted to name him Andrew, but he heard the Lord tell him "Michael, call him Michael." Later that day, while I was watching the children, I went into labor, went to the hospital and, hours later, gave birth to Michael. Michael always had a tender heart, and he was very sweet. However, he has a warrior type personality.

When he was born, they wheeled me out of the room and the Spirit of God hit me with the spirit of laughter. We thought we were having no more children, but the Lord said I would have one more.

Matthew was next, as the youngest and was one of Agnes' favorites. As a baby he would stay with her at night. He always ate the candy from her candy buckets. When she preached, he would be right there by her side. They had a special bond, and you could see the impartation. He couldn't live hiding things, and he would always have to confess something if it wasn't right. He started to read at four years old, and he would read the King James Bible. He could read a book like this very quickly and understand it.

My children went to a Christian school where they didn't even charge us tuition. We had to drive for nearly an hour to take them and return each morning and another hour to pick them up each afternoon. In addition, there were sports practices, events, and school events and it was a lot to do. I was also speaking and ministering, I had a good feeling about another Christian school that was closer. One day, I felt like I should go in and speak to them. When we talked, they said they had a burden to help us and felt our children should go to their school.

For five years I oversaw their study hall, and Jamie would substitute sometimes when teachers were out. It was a school that went up to 12th grade and was a wonderful provision for our children's education.

JAMES & DIANE
PROFET

FAMILY

Chapter 24
Kings Ranch

We were at the village, near Vicente Guererro, Mexico living in our bus with our five children and ministering to the people.

One day Jamie said, "I feel like I need to go to Sommer Haven.

When Jamie arrived, there was a group of people going to King's Ranch and they asked Jamie to go with them. As he went, he heard the voice of the Lord say, "I'm going to put you here." The Kings Ranch is a ministry center situated on 45 acres located in rural Kings County, California. It has a main building with kitchen, dining room, meeting room, and offices and has cottages for visitors or staff and has dormitories and a multi-purpose building and shop building. We fully moved to the facility just before Christmas 1995.

I had been conducting vacation Bible school at the village in Mexico and went to the laundromat to use their phone to call Sommer Haven. There was no electricity or phone where we lived in the village, so I went to the laundromat to call Sister Agnes, and she told me that Jamie had been voted to be the director for Kings Ranch. I was so surprised.

When we first arrived at the King's Ranch, we sensed the need for spiritual cleansing because of events that had taken place there in the past. The Lord led us to do a Jericho march—walking around the property daily. In the beginning, we planned to walk for seven days, but my son felt strongly that we should walk for eight days.

During that time, the weather was thick with fog, and the sun did not appear. But on the eighth and final day, we experienced a powerful breakthrough. The clouds began to part, and the sun broke through. As it did, every building on the property seemed to glow like gold. Something shifted in the atmosphere, it was a very precious time.

So, I transitioned from Mexico to King's Ranch and began working alongside my husband to start up the ministry there. But my heart was sad—we had planned to go to Guatemala in the jungles to work with the women there. It was just so strong in my heart. I found myself pouting and praying, "Lord, I know my husband heard Your voice... but I don't feel anything in my heart for this place."

Then, there was a group that arrived at our door.

When they knocked, we opened the door and they said, "We heard about you." They were boys from Guatemala, and some from El Salvador. We invited them in, and the power of God fell on them.

One particular boy was on the floor weeping, the Lord said to me, "Diane, you would not have chosen this, but I have, and I will bring the nations to you, and I will impart to them, and they will go back to the nations, empowered by my spirit, and they will do the greater works." He said, "Even the religious people will say, where did these people come from?"

You see these boys were from the gangs. They were young men that had been through so much, yet no one would expect them to serve God. And God changed their lives. Well, I immediately yielded to the Lord.

The Lord told us to bring them in. Within a few months, we had 12 young men under the age of 18. They came out of the gangs and wanted Jesus Christ. Well, what do you do with 12 young men under the age of 18?

You start a school.

Chapter 25

King's Ranch - ACE School

We took in some young boys who had been in the gangs. We had about 12 of them at one time, and we had to start a school to teach them because they were all under 18. We also had five children of our own, and we had missionary families who would also live with us. I went through Accelerated Christian Education (ACE) for training to be certified to start a school at King's Ranch.

The Lord brought in a principal for us who was a retired teacher. She and I, along with some others, went for the training at ACE. When we got there, we were taking the test and literally, because of my disabilities, I didn't have the capacity to comprehend much. I went through that training and at times would run to the bathroom and cry, saying, "God, I can't do this."

Then a miracle happened; I felt Jesus come into my body. He came in like a gentle wind and said, "I'm going to do the test. Don't worry. And after you're done with it, I'm going to give you the revelation of what you just took." He took my hand; he took the test, and I passed. I passed because He did it.

I put the school in operation, and the Lord continued giving it to me by revelation. I would just know the right answers and directions. It just came to me like revelation knowledge! Most of my life has been that way. I have totally depended on God's revelation. It's what leads me.

I believe that's something that the Lord would like to do with every believer. He says we have the mind of Christ. A lot of times our own understanding and our own mind gets in the way and prevents us from hearing what He has to say. As educated or as intelligent as we may be, we can never have the knowledge of God on a human level. He's always so much more. However, we can spend our entire lives taking in His teachings and learning as much as we can.

We had a board member who shared his testimony that he was a Methodist pastor who knew the Bible, went to school, but didn't know God. But one day God visited him, and he truly got born again which changed his whole ministry. You can learn so much from books and lectures, but that's just head knowledge. You can know the Bible, preach, teach, and even lead a church — and still not truly know God. Because it's not about information; it's about a relationship. It's about knowing God and allowing Him to reveal Himself to you. I base most of my education on spiritual things, because God deposits it, and then He brings it by revelation.

I always said to the Lord, "God, I don't want to just know scripture; I want to know You. I want to live that way." There's a difference between knowing and living and walking in Him. It was so amazing that God did that for me while I was studying to be a teacher.

I was teaching twelve young people, plus my own children, and we also had volunteer teachers that came in. I had to learn it first, just how to operate the program, to illustrate it, to demonstrate it, to make it a reality of the school. So, that's what I did. When I was at Sommer Haven, I worked with the preschoolers. Geri, the head teacher, taught me the Montessori program. Then I would teach the young ones Montessori. This also helped me teach those who were at our school at Kings Ranch.

This revelation knowledge affected other areas of my life. It made such a difference. When I came to Sommer Haven, I didn't really have a lot of knowledge, but I learned how to cook. I was never taught how to cook by my mother, so I had to learn. It took a lot of burnt and cut fingers, but with determination, I learned. You know, it's not an easy task to feed a hundred people.

I was taught how to cook, and it has benefited me in so many ways. God used what I learned in the natural to help me minister in the spiritual. Now, we host many groups where I feed a lot of people, and I need to determine how much food to cook for them.

That's where Teresa's teaching on multiplication helped me. I oversaw the food ministry. Teresa worked with me by revelation. It's like a light turned on that was never there before. The training was by the Holy Spirit. Yet it was in very natural and practical things, which is so important. We may go to Bible school, and we may get head knowledge, but we need to be able to work it into our lives in a natural way.

That's what was so beautiful about being trained by the Spirit of the Lord, because the natural and the spiritual flow together.

We see many people preach in the pulpit without godly character, and it's heartbreaking. There's something about working faithfully in the natural that shapes our character in ways that wouldn't happen otherwise, especially when we must press in through the Spirit. It produces spiritual determination and integrity. It creates a spiritual determination and integrity that only comes through that process.

A lot of spiritual breakthroughs come by pressing into faithfulness in the natural realm.

Agnes would say, **"Do a job that you don't like to do. Do it. It will change your life."** And it's true. I teach, I work with a lot of young people, and I instill values in them. Values that have never been instilled in their lives before. It's beautiful because they wouldn't get it otherwise just by going through Bible School. I've seen those who have submitted in the natural, and there's a big difference. It really builds the character of Christ in you. Christ is not so interested in our head knowledge, but He is interested in a willing and the teachable spirit.

Sometimes head knowledge brings pride and pride brings a fall. Through many years of ministry, I've seen a lot of people go so far in Christ but hold back in one area. Being unteachable or prideful can be a downfall.

It's not so much how we start the race, but it is how we finish the race that matters.

> "Pride *goes* before destruction, and a haughty spirit before stumbling."
>
> — Proverbs 16:18

After a few years of working with the boys, the Lord led them in different directions, some into ministry, others into professional careers. One of them even became a doctor and wrote us a letter, thanking us for what he had received during his time with us.

To God be the glory!

KINGS RANCH

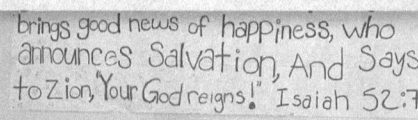

brings good news of happiness, who announces Salvation, And Says to Zion, "Your God reigns!" Isaiah 52:7

Chapter 26
A New Dimension

After the young men went on to other places, the Lord said to close the doors because He was going to visit us. That was in early 2001, and as the visitation unfolded, the ministry shifted into another dimension - another expression. In those three months of visitation, the Lord did something that was very new to us.

First, He said to me, "I want you to lie on this couch and be still." That was so hard—we were always on the move, constantly doing ministry. But I chose to yield to the process. Then He spoke again: "I'm going to do a surgery in you. I will remove what is not of Me. Whatever you think you have—place it on a shelf—and I will sort it out. What is not of Me will be taken out, and what is of Me will remain."

That process took three months.

It was a time when the glory of God would come down and I couldn't even hardly walk. God took me into another dimension, and He began to teach me many things. Things that later I found was also happening to others in the body of Christ. God was moving His people into the prophetic. It was a different realm.

The presence of God came to abide even stronger at Kings Ranch. "I'm going to use this as a spiritual hospital. Many of My people are bound and sick, and they need this. This will be a stronghold for the Kingdom of God, where I will minister to My people."

Jamie and I direct the ministry, but it is God who leads. He is the One who pours out His Spirit and does the work in people. We simply assist Him—but He is the One.

We began to move in a different way—even in my husband's worship. His worship started to change. We no longer just sang the usual Christian songs; God began giving Jamie visions, and as he sang those visions, people would fall under the power of God.

Visitors would have encounters with the Lord. They would receive deliverance and healing. People would fall under the power, and we thought "Oh my gosh, we are putting everyone to sleep." We did not realize that God was pouring out Himself on the people.

You know how, in Genesis, God put Adam to sleep and took out his rib? In a similar way, God was putting people into a place of rest—removing things, ministering to them—and they were having powerful encounters with Him, even non-believers. One man came and said that God took him up into heavenlies. We experienced this many times. Well, Jamie just didn't understand, and he said, "I'm just putting everybody to sleep."

"Come on, everybody, wake up." Jamie said. Then the Lord told Jamie, "I'm doing a surgery in people's lives." We experienced a different dimension—one that healed people and brought them into a place of rest where they could hear God and a new clarity in the spirit.

After the three-month period the Lord opened the doors again and a Baptist pastor asked if he could bring his congregation. We prayed, "Lord, is this of you?" Not everyone is prepared to receive. The Lord said, "Yes." While they were with us, the pastor's son asked me to pray for him, the power of the Lord came, and he was on the floor.

Before we knew it, there was a line of children, and everyone that came from his congregation ended up on the floor. The pastor was pacing back and forth, troubled, because he wasn't Pentecostal but what was so unique was that God's glory came in such a way that the children did not get up. They had to be carried to their cars. It was truly a demonstration of God's presence and glory.

About 20 years later, one of the children that we prayed for came back and said, "I just had to come and tell you that I have never felt God in such a way as I felt that day when I was 5 years old and it changed my life."

We thank God for His presence that touches lives.

Chapter 27
The Altar

"Then the Spirit took me up and brought me into
the inner courtyard, and the glory of the LORD
filled the Temple."

— Ezekiel 43:5

At the time, we had a young woman named Diana with us. She said the Lord had told her to come and stay for six months—she ended up staying for six years. The Lord also brought her husband into her life during that time, and my husband and I had the honor of officiating their wedding in 2001. Diana and Javier stayed with us for six years.

Later, the Lord put it on Diana's heart to host a 20th Anniversary Celebration for us, which was called "The Gathering of the Eagles." At the end of the six years God sent Diana, Javier and their son back to Chihuahua, Mexico as missionaries.

During the time Diana was with us, we had a living room in the main building. The Lord instructed Diana to create an altar in that room, and that altar remains there to this day. God began to move, and we started to enhance the space. He would guide us— "Place this here, put that there"—and as we followed His direction, His presence began to dwell there.

He told me, "Put water fountains because I am the living waters." And when people go there, they would experience God in the deeper depths of His presence, as if they stood before Him. People came and lay in that space and received healing and deliverance. At times, we didn't even pray for people. God himself liberated them.

I thank God for Diana and Javier; they were a big part of that move of God. Now, God is using them in Mexico and for many years we would go and visit them. God continues to pour out His Spirit in the remote areas, in Chihuahua, in the mountains, among the Indians, and wherever they go, God is glorified in their lives.

Many people desired the experience they received from the Lord, that deposit that they took with them. God deposits His Spirit within people and sends them back to their people carrying the impartation. What God is doing is beautiful.

THE ALTAR

Chapter 28
A New Kind of Worship

A woman took one of Jamie's music CDs to Australia. There was a man from Africa who heard the music and was touched by it. He asked for a CD and I gave him one. Later he asked if it was okay to use the CD in his country. He translated the songs into his language. Many people love to worship, but they don't know how to enter into God's deep place, His stillness. It's in that stillness where you can receive so much from the Lord. This African brother took the music and began to teach his people, and it shifted his church. It brought the church into a place where God's presence would dwell.

When Sister Felistus from Zambia came in 2005 and 2007, she experienced the stillness too - that depth of God's rich presence, and she also took what she learned back to her church. She said people would feel God's presence after she had been to the ministry center. She said it became another 'King's Ranch.' People would come and they learned to wait on God; they learned to seek Him and to come into His dimension. When we're aligned with God's will, we connect with God in a different, beautiful way.

We went into people's homes, and they would play that music; they played it even outside on speakers. It was nothing that we invented, planned or thought of; it was just something God began to breathe on.

So, God began to breathe His Spirit through that ministry of music, and we are touching the nations. We still are, today.

Chapter 29
Benjamin

I'll never forget the time when my son Benjamin was about 11 years old, we found ourselves deep in prayer, enveloped by a powerful sense of intercession. We didn't fully understand what we were praying for—only that we were being led to lift someone up in faith.

That day, I was at home and went over to the main ministry building about 70 yards away. When I arrived, a man was standing there, looking lost. As I approached him, the spirit of prophecy stirred within me, and words poured out: "You were just about to take your own life." His eyes widened in shock. "How did you know?" he asked, his voice trembling. He explained that an unseen force had taken over his hands as he drove, guiding him to our ministry center.

In that moment, I began to minister to him, sharing words of hope and life. He received them with an open heart, and I witnessed the transformative power of God unfold before my eyes. Later I recalled Sister Agnes once telling me that my husband Jamie and I would see God move in extraordinary ways—ways few others would ever experience. To me, this was a profound demonstration of the supernatural hand of God at work.

I had just finished a women's conference.

I had been invited to be the main speaker at a women's conference in Southern California. That women's conference in September 2008 was amazing. Many women were getting delivered at the altar. It was a moving of the Holy Spirit. I remember I felt like I was soaring in the Spirit.

I returned home to Kings Ranch, and that's when the Lord gave me an open vision. He said, "One of your sons will be leaving this world," but He didn't show me who it was. He said, "It's not how long we live on the earth that's important; it's where we end up." He said, "Except the seed dies; it will not bear fruit." I wrote it down and cried for hours. For days, I couldn't even talk to Jamie to tell him what I had seen. My eyes had been open; it was an open vision.

I told God that I just needed to know that the child would be in heaven with Him. That's all I needed to know. And I said, "But can I intercede, Lord? Can I intercede?"

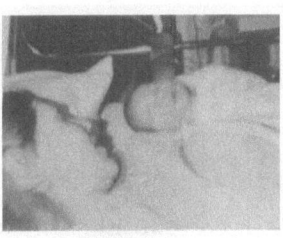

Benjamin at birth

He said, "It's already settled, this will happen."

So, I yielded and said, "I give him to You."

One of the most difficult things for a mother is to see one of her children die. It is very painful. Even though the Lord told me, it still took a lot of time for me to process. There was a knowing in me that I could not change what God had showed me.

It was a supernatural way that the Lord brought me through that time, July 1st, 2011, when we found out our 25-year-old son, Benjamin, had taken his own life. That night like many nights, we would watch him because he took medication for mental illness. I had just asked if he had taken his medicine. It's a long story, but I will just share what happened that night, I won't go into all of it, maybe another time.

So, I remember that night he came and kissed me. He said, "I love you, Mom."

Not only then, but days before that, he put his head on my lap and he said, "Mom," and then he started confessing things in his life; he really asked the Lord to forgive him. You know, he really did cry out for God to give him back his mind.

Benjamin had slipped into a dark place and didn't know how to get out of it. Sometimes when we walk away from God, there are consequences. I know God could have brought him out of it, but there are things we don't understand and things I don't question. I don't want to question either because then you start blaming God.

So, that morning, like we normally would, we went to check on him. He wasn't there. Then, we went looking for him, where he normally would be. Jamie called the police and let them know that we were missing someone that had been feeling suicidal and was not in the right frame of mind.

In the morning, we heard a fire engine, but we didn't realize that it was for our Benjamin. Then the investigator came, and he asked us what he was wearing. We gave him the details and then he looked at us and said, well, "I'm sorry to tell you, but your son took his life this morning." There was something deep, still deep in my heart, that he would make it through. I really didn't know that Benjamin would be the one. You just kind of get into shock, it's terrible.

I had the horrible task of calling up the children and letting them know what happened. And then after I called the last one a peace flooded my heart. I looked at the investigator and I said, "It's okay, I have peace now." It was as if I was on the chest of Jesus. Literally on the chest of Jesus. And still my mind was processing things, but somehow, I experienced the presence of God. Many people started coming from all over.

People were praying all through the night. It's as if the presence of the Lord increased even deeper. I know there were quite a few people there, I don't even know who was there. However, I began to minister to them and comfort them. Only God could do that.

It was something supernatural. I know that God's presence really increased in that time, it was such a depth of compassion. Since then, God has opened doors for me to minister to so many people that have lost their children the same way. It's as if God imparts His peace to them. The week after the funeral, Jamie and I went and ministered to youth in Bakersfield.

The Lord told us that there was a mantle that we needed to pick up in the Spirit, that was Benjamin's, and we were going to give it to this generation. In that meeting, the Spirit of God began to manifest Himself in a beautiful way to the youth in that service. From there we

headed to Mexico....to
Cuauhtémoc, in Chihuahua,
Mexico.

There are times, when I was
not ministering to others, that
I would feel deep emotions.
There were times when I
processed things. Do you
know what I mean? It's not
like I didn't cry, but at certain
times God would supernaturally hold me. I would still be
processing. It is a process that you must go through.

The death of Benjamin was such a shock, but a
supernatural peace just flooded me. At that time, I felt
as if I was leaning on the chest of Jesus constantly.
Experiencing that trauma helped me realize that God
had supernaturally given me peace, He had visited me
already and had told me that one of my children was
leaving.

Sometimes, we don't
understand why the Lord
works in the ways he does. I
would ask Him, "Why are you
taking my son?" But it was
something that He already
knew and allowed. Maybe
Benjamin was the seed that
had to die.

It had been several years prior that I somehow knew something like this would happen.

> Verily, verily, I say unto you, **Except a grain of wheat fall into the earth and die**, it abideth by itself alone; but if it die, it beareth much fruit.
>
> — John 12:24

We drove from California to Cuauhtémoc, Mexico to do ministry in late July 2011, shortly after Ben had died. After our long trip, we rested, and while I was sleeping, I had a dream. It was more than a dream – it was a visitation from God. I was sleeping, and it was very real.

In the dream, Jamie and I were trying to get a car started. Our late son, Benjamin, appeared, and he got in the car, and he started it. Once the car started, Jamie and I got back into the car and Benjamin came to the window. I rolled down the window and Benjamin said, "Mom, "Do you see this maze?" He showed me a picture of a maze that led to a lighthouse. He said, "Mom, I made it to the lighthouse. Thank you for all your prayers." Then he said to me, "There are three things the Lord is commissioning you to do on the earth. You will find out what they are, and God will be leading you and speaking to you about what they are."

The glow that was on Benjamin was so beautiful. He glowed and radiated the presence of the Lord. God's presence was so strong, that even when I woke up, God's presence was still in the room. I shared this with Jamie and those that were with us. They also began to feel that presence of the Lord.

As I began to share, God lifted our spirits in a beautiful way.

Another time after we went back to the ministry center, a prophet from Germany visited us. And she said, "I see your son with the heavenly host."

I also received a prophetic song through Kimberly and Alberto Riviera, who are worshippers. They personally sang to me this word from the Lord, "I see the heavenly host cheering you on." The words just felt connected.

Again, three months after Ben's death I went to a women's conference and met the speaker, Retha McPherson, who is from South Africa. She was praying for people, and she came and laid hands on me. She prophesied to me and said, "You have sown a very expensive seed, and through that very expensive seed, you will see the harvest." Amen.

I knew that expensive seed was my precious Benjamin.

Chapter 30
God's Provision

Anytime we needed food, God would send someone with food. We never lacked, and the Lord always provided. I remember during Christmas of 1993 we received a donation of about a thousand gifts. We made many candy and food bags full of food that people had donated. We would go to different stores, and they would donate. Through the donations, we were able to feed around 70 children a week in Mexicali. We were so involved. We had maybe 15 turkeys donated, and we cooked them. We also had a bus, so we would cook food and take it to the poorest areas and feed the people. We would give out candy bags and presents. We were so busy all the time doing that. The day that Christmas came, I realized I did not even get gifts for my children! I was just so involved in giving to others.

But God... An elderly couple living in El Centro came, and they had beautiful gifts...big, beautiful gifts for my children. They said the Lord had burdened their hearts to come and bring those gifts. The faithfulness of God shined through many people.

The income we have now, is still the provision that God gives. Since we've been here, we've almost never been late with a bill. Our bills get paid, sometimes at the last moment, which is not a small thing because we live on a 47-acre ranch. Large facilities, dormitories, and many areas there include a lot of bills like electricity. I can't tell you how or what because we never charge. The only offerings that we ask for are for missions, not for ourselves or our ministry.

It is amazing how God has provided for us. One time in about 1997, when Jamie was in the office, we needed to pay a bill. Jamie began crying, "God, have I done anything wrong?" You always check yourself to make sure your heart is right with God. The Lord spoke to me and said, "It's coming." So, I walked downstairs and there was a woman there. She said, "Hi, I want to give you this." She wrote out a check, and it paid the bill. God always works in wonderful and mysterious ways.

We had all those boys, and we were teaching them while schooling our own children. How would we buy their schoolbooks and supplies? God had amazing way of providing.

One time someone fell asleep driving on the road, and they ran into our fence with their car and even hit a tree. They were fine and got out without a scratch, but their insurance had to pay the necessary funds to replace the fence. Well, that money paid for all the materials we needed and the fence never got rebuilt.

People would just come, sent by the Lord. I remember one time that a woman who was just driving by who said she was from Texas, and said that the Lord told her to stop, come into the building, and leave a check for us. So, she stopped, came in, and said, "The Lord told me to leave a check here." We didn't even know who she was.

It has been over 40 years that God has provided for us. I also remember when our car had gone out on us, and we needed a new car. Someone approached me and said, just meet us at the car lot and pick out the car you need. That's the car we have now, and we're very thankful for it. They paid cash right there on the spot. It is amazing because through the ministry, we support missions in Zambia, Mexico, Ecuador, China, and India. So, out of the ministry, as we live by faith, we also give to others.

There is a man that's been very precious and sometimes he gives to the ministry. We said, "We just want to thank you for your offering." The man replied, "I want to thank you — because I don't know where I would be if I hadn't come to King's Ranch." He came to King's Ranch where he was delivered from drugs. He and his wife had filed papers for divorce. When his wife visited, there was such a separation. The spirit of prophecy came on me and said, "The Lord says you guys are going to be closer than you ever have been." Then they found out they were never divorced; the paperwork never went through! Now they have a very strong marriage. He said he would not be here today if God had not brought him to us.

One day the Lord gave us a word that He would always provide for us. He gave us a word through a prophet that God would even provide vacation time for us. People have approached us and said, "We want to pay and send you to a resort." They blessed us by paying for everything. We even got to go on a cruise. We have not even desired those things, but the Lord has blessed us.

One time, in 1997, I got a suitcase for my birthday, and I jokingly said, "All I need now is a ticket to Hawaii." Two weeks later, a friend called and said, "Can you guys get away for two weeks?"

I said, "I don't know."

She responded, "Well, the Lord burdened me to pay for a ticket for you guys to go to Hawaii." By the time we were leaving, the Lord had put a thousand dollars in our hands for the trip. We were able to go to the main part of Hawaii, and we also flew to Kona, on the big Island. We had the money to fly, and in Kona we connected with a pastor from Canada and, a few years later, ended up ministering in his church in British Columbia. It was a divine connection.

On many of our trips, things start out one way and end up another. Another time, in 2018, we were in the Healing Rooms in Spokane, Washington, and we met a group of Japanese women. The Lord had us minister to them, and the glory of God came down. They all came under the power of the Holy Spirit. They invited us to come minister in Japan which we did the following year. The Lord's presence was with us.

Speaking in El Salvador

In 2002, a young man from Taiwan needed much deliverance from demons that had affected his mind. When talking with him on the phone, the Spirit of the Lord came upon Jamie and told him to come as fast as he could. He came and stayed for 2 weeks. The Lord delivered him, set him free, and then gave him spiritual gifts. God deposits His gifts into people. That day he received the gift of prophecy and still exercises it today.

Later, after he married and had children, he would visit us at the ministry quite often. We are his mother and father in the Lord, and his children call us grandma and grandpa. Now he runs a ministry that sponsors missionaries from other countries. He was inspired by an elderly Taiwanese man to translate. So, he translates writings and recordings from English into Mandarin and vice versa.

One day in 2017, I was sitting in my home and the Lord said, "I am sending you to Tawain." The next day this young man called and invited us to minister on a cruise ship that was going to be chartered in September to circumnavigate Taiwan for two days for worship, prayer, prophetic declarations, and an evangelistic rally on a small island belonging to Taiwan. There were 1,800 intercessors onboard and 24-hour prayer and worship for those days. Only intercessors were on the cruise. Over the days of the cruise, they were reading the entire Bible and worshipping and praying over all the islands. Many of the Christian indigenous Taiwanese people also came on the cruise.

It's amazing how the Lord provided for us to do that. Christians came together to pray and worship. We prayed, had meetings and ministered. Our sessions brought deliverance and healing.

This is just how God works.

This is just how God works. We travelled to other places in Taiwan after the cruise, ministering among the people.

> "All the ends of the earth will remember and turn
>   to the Lord, and all the families of the nations
>   will worship before You."

> — Psalm 22:27 NIV

TAIWAN

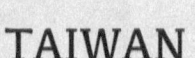

TAIWAN

Chapter 31
Cancer

In the summer of 2021, I brought a young woman for her doctor's appointment, and while I was there, I just felt in my heart that I should make a dentist appointment. So, I did. I went in and they did an examination, took x-rays, and then made an appointment for teeth cleaning. I went in and saw a very precious African American dentist and he said, "When you came in the last time, this bump was not there; you need to see a specialist as soon as possible." It turned out that I had a tumor on the roof of my mouth. I noticed a little something before, but I just didn't pay attention. I called the specialist, and they said it would take three months before I got in.

Then I called the dentist back, he said, "Let me make some phone calls." He got me in immediately. Then he said, "I'd like you to do a follow-up. Let me know what's happening. If there's any problem, let me know." He was very precious. I went for that appointment, and I kind of already knew something was wrong. However, I had perfect peace. When the doctor came in, they said they needed to have a biopsy. I asked if they thought it was cancer. He told me yes. So, I replied, "Don't worry. I'm okay. Because God is with me." Even during terrible news, I knew God was with me.

The biopsy was very painful. He told me, "I'm really impressed how you could keep your mouth open for that period of time." It took two weeks to get the results. So, when I went to the next appointment, they said it was cancer, and it was a very aggressive cancer, that moves very quickly. He told me there was a surgical procedure to remove the tumor and they also wanted me to have radiation.

It was beautiful because every time I went in, the presence of God would just fill the room. Before you knew it, the doctors were all coming in and they knew God was there. They could feel Him. Then, I had to do an MRI to image the cancer, and they also wanted to schedule me for surgery. I was in danger of losing some of my vocal cords. After that I had to decide if I was going to have the surgery. I had known a pastor that had breast cancer, and she didn't want to get checked. She didn't want to go through the procedure, and she ended up dying.

I had every viewpoint you could possibly think of. Jamie knew that there could be very bad side effects, so he wasn't too fond of the surgery. Then Mariela, one of my spiritual daughters, cried and told me that I needed to get the surgery and I decided to go through with it.

A precious sister named Estela Plata who I do ministry with, is called a miracle woman. She's had cancer three times. God told her to come be with me, so she flew from Houston, Texas. She was such a blessing. Different people came just to be there with me.

Although they couldn't be there for the surgery, they came before and were there afterward. So, she came and prayed for me along with others. Jamie was having a very difficult time since he really didn't want me to get the surgery. In the midst of it all, I heard the Lord say, "This is for my glory." So, I said, "I'm having the surgery."

Then Jamie replied, "Are you sure you're having the surgery?" The side effects were losing your voice, etc. But the alternative is cancer. To me, there was no choice, I had to have the surgery.

The morning of the surgery, he woke up crying and told me the Lord had told him that it is all for His glory. I had a vision of Jesus at a surgery table, behind the surgeon. So, I found the picture and personally gave it to the surgeon. It was during the time of COVID, so nobody could go with me. They just dropped me off. It was such a lonely time going in by myself, through the doors, but I knew I wasn't alone.

I went in and I handed the picture to the doctor. He said, "Thank you." He still tells me to this day that he has that picture. Throughout the entire situation, I just had a lot of peace, a real strong peace. It was supposed to be outpatient surgery. Can you believe that? In and out. When they started, they had to have like seven surgeons there. They say that the surgery was not a little surgery. During the surgery, I began to bleed, and I bled a lot. I ended up in the hospital for five days, but the Lord used me the entire time.

I had so much pain. They had to put a feeding tube in so that I could eat. I had bled so much that I was vomiting a lot of blood. I didn't have any communication with Jamie because I didn't bring my phone, since I thought I was going to get out the same day. I couldn't even get up out of bed and had to use a bedpan. I knew that I wasn't going to be released from the hospital, unless I could eat.

I felt a strength within my spirit. I looked at the nurse and said, "Can I walk to the bathroom?" She said, "I'll teach you how to unhook the infusion machine and pull it with you." And she did. From that time on, I began to improve. I immediately started praying for her. There were other people I prayed for as well. The nurse just began to weep. The Lord touched her. Jamie was able to get a phone to me through talking to the nurse, so I was able to communicate. It seemed a lot better because I could feel the spiritual support.

I was only able to talk a little because I couldn't really open my mouth, so I had a hard time communicating what I needed. They were feeding me pudding, and I could hardly stomach chocolate, but I knew if I wanted out of that hospital, I had to do it. Don't ask me how I did it, but I did it. I got out of the hospital, and then I came home.

There was a team of people waiting for me. The Lord had Sister Minni come and help me and she is an ICU nurse. Pastor Rosalinda came, a woman who has been like a mother to me. Everyone was just so good to me. They offered me regular food, but I had to eat pureed food without any spices, as anything else would burn my mouth.

They removed much more tissue than they had expected, because by the time I received the surgery, the tumor had grown. They also took out some of my upper jawbone. They had to take and put a plastic thing and cover it with my skin. So, that's why there were so many surgeons.

When I came home, I couldn't open my mouth. It was very difficult.

I really lost a lot of weight since I couldn't hardly stomach anything, but my spirits were up. When people came to visit me, the presence of God was so powerful that they left touched and ministered to.

About two or three weeks later, I went to my follow-up appointment. This doctor kept coming in and out, in and out. Finally, she came in, and she said, "You're the one."

She said, "I can't imagine how you look so good after the surgery that you had. That's why I kept coming in and out. I thought I had the wrong room." I was able to testify and share that it is God and the power of prayer.

Then I had to go to therapy to learn to open my mouth. I had to use popsicle sticks to pry my mouth open because otherwise I couldn't open it. They wanted me to do it every two hours. It was painful, but you must keep it open. Therapy was tough, but God was always good.

During the surgery, they had to keep taking specimens to make sure there's no cancer. So, when they took it all, I guess they found out that there was cancer very close to where they cut. So, now they said I had to have radiation, and they wanted to give me like 30 radiation treatments in my mouth, which would have really damaged me. I don't know if I would have been able to even talk. The specialist had said that this was what I needed. They were very concerned about cancer because you have to move very quickly.

All at once a couple approached me, and they said, "We want to pay for you to go to the Oasis of Hope hospital in Tijuana, Mexico." They gave me a check for about $24,000.

After about six weeks, I called the Oasis of Hope. It is a well-known alternative treatment cancer hospital that treats cancer without chemotherapy. People from all over the world go there. I sent all my records, and they said, "come," so I went.

It was amazing. The doctors pray with you and give you IVs like vitamin C. While you're sitting in the chair, they're worshipping and preaching. The presence of God is very strong in the hospital. We ministered to many, touching people from all over the world. They take your blood, and when they put it back in you; they give you certain treatments that alert your body to target tumors for cancer.

I went there and had a lot of treatments, even though I was very weak, I improved, and the treatments helped me. They taught me how to eat, how to use organic foods, and how to eliminate sugar from my diet because it causes cancer. They gave me videos about how to change my diet. You eat very little meat and no dairy products. You eat plant-based food like quinoa, beans, vegetables but a minimal number of fruits. They give you classes and everything.

After that, I went back to the doctor who wanted to give me radiation, and he talked to me. They wanted me to just go and see him, so I did. He told me that I could have a million cancer cells floating around my head right now. He looked at me and said, "You should immediately have come for these treatments." At first, I did not tell him I went down to Mexico, but then I told him. He looked at me again, and he said, "Well, wherever your peace is, go with that."

All my doctors and surgeons were so precious, because they would all check in on me when I came. It was like the presence of God would just come. I don't know how to explain it, but they would feel such hope. Maybe they saw hope in me, since many of the patients don't make it.

The Oasis doctors recommended that I return after a year for another maintenance treatment of the Dendritic Cell Vaccine. Some friends and family said that they wanted to pay for it and this time it was about $13,000 for the treatment. The Lord provided, again, for my treatment. I did not ask anyone but the Lord, and the Lord provided.

Like with my son Benjamin, I felt as if I was leaning on the chest of Jesus, this was no different. With this cancer experience, I felt like He was my provider and healer. The Lord provides every time. The Lord showed me, that even in my personal needs, He was there for me.

Jesus carried me through this time in my life. I felt His presence through it all and ministered to a lot of people while I was there. God used me for His greater good.

Even while at the Oasis, people would come to my room to talk and pray. It's like people know there's something different about a Spirit filled person. They knew we were ministers and were praying for people, and that was very beautiful.

After the second visit to the Oasis Hospital, everything was clear, and I feel well today. I do still have some pain in my mouth, and it feels like something is there all the time, but it is just something that I live with. I can speak, chew, and swallow normally but I do have to be careful how much I eat and how I swallow my food. People do not even know because I look normal, but I do live with some side effects of the surgery. You learn to live and be content and thankful just because God is God and he is good.

OASIS OF HOPE
HOSPITAL

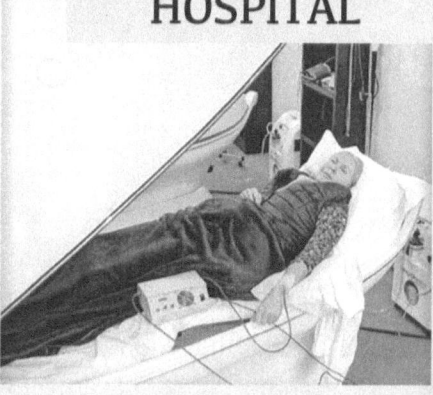
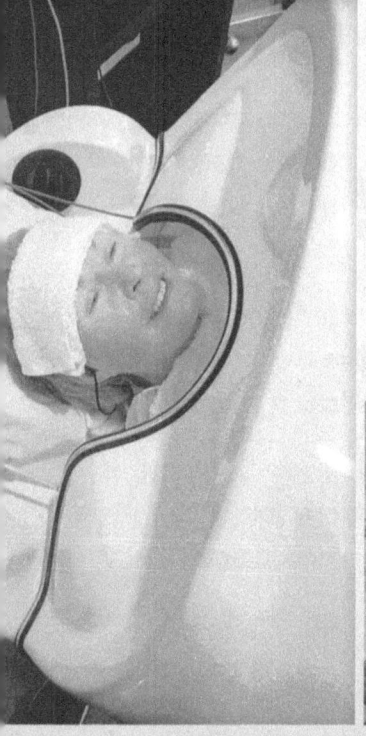

Chapter 32
The Faithfulness of God

I am so grateful for the many ways God moved in my life through challenges, even through cancer. A lot of times I just think that God uses doctors. You do not need to feel like you have less faith if you must go to a doctor. I needed to go through this process, due to having cancer, but God was glorified in the midst of it by the peace and divine presence that the doctors could feel. They told me that a lot of times people don't make it through. Jamie knew someone that had a similar cancer who had the surgery and took all the radiation treatments and died later. I think the radiation killed him.

However, the Lord said to me, "This is for My glory." What was beautiful was that I had no fear at all, at any time. God is so good and faithful to His servants.

Through all my ordeal so many people came to lift me up and encourage me and pray for me. A precious sister gave me a prophetic word that greatly encouraged me. I am so thankful to everyone who has been a part of my life who helped me and encouraged me in the challenges of recovering from the surgery.

Chapter 33
My Day

We never advertise or try to promote the Kings Ranch ministry. It's always been promoted by word of mouth by those who come and are deeply touched. Because their lives have been touched or transformed, they go and tell others. If they're from another country, they often want people from their own nation to come and experience what they've encountered. It's all happened through word of mouth—through lives that have been changed and a desire to see others experience the same freedom they've found.

My day consists of people, cooking, cleaning, mentoring, teaching and prayer. Prayer and just being in the quiet place of His presence. This is not always easy and requires constant communion with the Lord.

We work with churches and pastors. The pastors look to us to help their people. We're always there, doing ministry, delivering, healing, teaching, feeding people, of course, and all the natural things that come along with the ministry. Like Agnes said, we learn to walk in the Spirit. When you're in the Spirit, you can do all things.

One of the things I learned from Sister Agnes, is to live and move and have our being in Him, to totally surrender. We become nothing, so He can come in and be everything and be glorified through our lives. People are looking for Jesus, and they must see Him in you. When you bring the nature of Christ, then others can tangibly see it and feel it. Living out your faith has more impact than just giving someone a tract. Like Agnes would say, we must become that living epistle.

This scripture has been one of my favorites:

> "But God hath chosen the foolish things of the world to confound the wise; and God hath chosen the weak things of the world to confound the things which are mighty;"
>
> — 1 Corinthians 1:27 KJV

To the world, I would be considered a foolish person. Especially since I was a girl who grew up with no direction in life, whose mother suffered hardships, her father died, was not a high school graduate, brother was in a gang... Yet, God took me because He knew my heart, and He gave me the privilege of placing me with Sister Agnes I. Numer, who was trained by Jesus. God used this to change my life and send me around the world, for His glory.

Sister Agnes asked me to come and live at Sommer Haven when she met me the first night. That first night, she prayed with me, and she asked me the first night. She had never met me before then. She did not know that I wanted so badly to be free and yield and be trained by the Holy Spirit. However, the Spirit of the Lord knew it. He put it on her heart to ask. You don't realize until you look back what God has done and what He's still doing. We are constantly in a process of becoming like Him.

I've seen a lot of people who have not finished the race. **My heart is to encourage you, no matter what difficulties, or problems, finish your race.** Sometimes we have an image of how our life will go or how our children are going to turn out. I would have never thought I would go through the things that I have gone through. However, it doesn't mean that God has forsaken us. It can mean that He has entrusted us to go through these things, and that we will not deny His name.

And suffering, we must embrace suffering.

This society doesn't want to embrace any suffering. It's blessings that they want. I'm telling you that in the work of the ministry, just as the apostles went through things, we will go through them too. But it's how we yield ourselves through them that qualifies us with God, by which He will know that He can entrust us with His glory.

Chapter 34
A Different Perspective

I first met Kathy Smith when she arrived at Sommer
Haven in July 1982 to be discipled in the Lord. We
became close friends back then and were drawn to each
other. She helped me realize things about myself. She
was a businesswoman, and I was a missionary, but we
had things in common. When you are part of God's
family, you will always have all things in common. We
have sweet fellowship with each other and spur one
another on to love and good works. I would like to share
some of the things that Kathy has shared with me in
hopes that it will encourage others in the ministry to stay
on the course.

*So, the thing that really stands out to me, Diane,
is I've watched you since we found each other
again, after several years, maybe five years. It's
that same quality I saw way back in 1982, which is
part of the reason I stayed at Sommer Haven. You*

*have a genuine, sweet, kind, and untainted spirit.
I would classify you as a person without guile.
Jesus used this word in the Bible about
Nathanael. So, I see that following you. That to
me is worth a zillion dollars. It is the peace that
resides in you, even though I'm in the business
world and you're in the missionary world, right?
So, you meet a lot of people, but I've noticed that
through all different situations and attitudes, you
don't get affected in the least bit.*

*With you, what stands out, again, is how you take
phone calls. It's rare if you don't take it, and you
only stop taking it during a prayer meeting, but
you always get back. That's an incredible quality
that is needed in the body of Christ, because for a
minister, you've got to be available. Somebody
could be dying, anything could happen, even
suicide. A minister must be on the go, must be
looking at their text messages, seeing.... and I've
noticed that about you. You're always available to
pray for somebody. When I call, a lot of times I'm
not even asking for prayer, I'm just talking, and
then you just start praying. Your life also involves
the flowing together of the natural and the
spiritual effortlessly and seamlessly. When you
are cooking, cleaning, and dealing with this
person or that, putting a party together, in all
things, you are flowing in and out of the natural
and the spiritual.*

Anybody else in that position would be probably complaining or whining, because it's a lot of hands-on. However, you don't complain. You could be praying in the Spirit for a whole church, to having to feed a large group of people. You don't whine and complain about things that don't go your way.

If you're faithful in those things, you're going to be faithful in much. The little things are still big with you. I see in you what I saw in Agnes in 1982 in New York. I remember saying, "This lady's got something," and I said, "She's got the authority and the ability." And that same quality is in you, Diane. It was deposited into you.

That was also part of what was deposited into you. The ability to pray for long periods of time - very few Christians will do that. Jesus said, "Go make disciples." So, it's just like a full package that God gave you when you sat at Agnes's feet and had no direction, no purpose to live.

You said you had no training, no nothing, no purpose, no direction. But yet, it's really amazing to me. It's the deposit that God placed in you through the person He chose to train you, that you now use in a worldwide ministry. So, whoever God puts us with, we need to really esteem and treasure that, because had you not sat still listening to the people before you, you might not have the ministry you have today.

— Kathy Smith

God has used these words to encourage me in the ministry I serve today. Put yourself around people who love and serve the Lord, and you will see their lives affect you and spur you on as well.

Chapter 35

God's People Need Peace

"Thou wilt keep him in perfect peace, whose mind
is stayed on thee: because he trusteth in thee.
Trust ye in the Lord for ever: for in the Lord
Jehovah is everlasting strength: For he
bringeth down them that dwell on high; the
lofty city, he layeth it low; he layeth it low, even
to the ground; he bringeth it even to the dust."

— Isaiah 26: 3-5 KJV

God's people need peace; you see that there's so much
out there that doesn't bring peace to people right? We
as Christians, can hold on to this scripture, and if we can
find someone like Sister Agnes to lead and guide us,
then we will be able to walk with Him. When I was with
Agnes, she would bring deliverance through the night
with me. Teresa had the patience to work with me and
saw that it wasn't rebellion when I did the opposite of
what she said. I just couldn't do it because I didn't have

the ability until God did a healing and restoration in my life. That's the deep part, because when your life is restored, then you want to see other's lives restored. We receive, so freely we give.

> "O Lord our God, other lords beside thee have had dominion over us: but by thee only will we make mention of thy name. 14 They are dead, they shall not live; they are deceased, they shall not rise: therefore hast thou visited and destroyed them, and made all their memory to perish."

> — Isaiah 26: 12-14 KJV

For me to take time ministering, this is my passion. Even if you minister to one person, it is worth it. Do we have any idea what a person connected to God can do? It's not in numbers, but in quality, and I think that it is very valuable to invest in a person's life. You must be wise because you want to invest in someone that you know is going to do something with what God has given.

> "Do not give what is holy to dogs, and do not throw your pearls before pigs, or they will trample them under their feet, and turn and tear you to pieces."

> — Matthew 7:6

You never know, sometimes the ones you thought would obey God's purpose for their lives are the very ones who don't—at least not right away. And the ones that you are not sure if they will obey God become great in His eyes. We must be patient and faithful to give, what God gives to us, to give. **It was with only twelve that Jesus reached the world.** We just have to keep our eyes on Him.

When the Lord shifted us to a new dimension, He said, "This is going to be a spiritual hospital." There have been many that have been in ministry that have fallen, but the Lord has used us to help restore them. We had a pastor that came from a large church in Mexico. He'd fallen into adultery, fallen into sin. Someone referred him to come, and the Lord restored him, restored his marriage, and when he went back, his ministry doubled.

There's a great need in the body of Christ. I have a heart to see people come to Christ, but I also have a heart to see people stay in Christ and be developed in God. We've just seen too many people fall away, that you would have never thought would have fallen.

Still, I know I haven't reached all that God has for me. Do you know what I mean? I know that we are just scratching the surface. I feel like it's just a drop in the bucket, even seeing everything that the Lord has done.

Agnes gave us a prophetic word. Agnes didn't give many words, but when she did, you knew it was from the Lord. She said, Jamie and I would see God move in ways that few had ever known. She gave us that word. She also said, "I see you with a lot of youth." And that is exactly what the Lord has done.

We've gone through a lot. I mean, personally, we've gone through a lot, but God has sustained us.

Maybe the message I can get to people is that no matter what it looks like, don't let go of God, and don't blame Him either.

> "What then shall we say to these things? If God *is* for us, who *is* against us?"
>
> — Romans 8:31 NASB

Chapter 36

May My Life be a Testimony

My life has not always been beautiful - there have been moments of sorrow and trials along with the moments of joy and gladness. But above all, God has reigned. He reigns over my past, over my present, and over my future. He has loved me through everything I've gone through. I trust Him because He's always faithful. My hope is that you may find His salvation and love in the midst of these words I've written. May my life be a testimony for many.

Your life is a testimony as well. It is a testimony that may include love, laughter, faith, trials, moments of every kind. You are the only one who gets to decide how to use your testimony.

May you take comfort in the words you've read and place your faith in the God who sees. He is the one who will bring you through until you see Him face to face.

"And the Lord is the one who is going ahead of

you; He will be with you. He will not desert you
or abandon you. Do not fear and do not be
dismayed."

— Deuteronomy 31:8

More Mission Journeys

GUATEMALA

- Guatemala - 1992

By James Profet

In June 1992, a Guatemalan pastor living East of Sommer Haven Ranch, with whom I had flown to Guatemala for 3 weeks the year before, had a burden to bring clothes and medications and a motorboat all the way to Guatemala. No big deal, just a 5000-kilometer drive on skinny, horrible, potholed highways across flooded rivers and washed-out roads in Mexican cartel territory, not to mention government checkpoints. It was difficult to tell who the terrorists were.

In retrospect, the trip was flawed from the start. Our Guatemalan pastor friend failed to do his homework and simply assumed that the old, worn-out, maintenance starved, motorboat he purchased for $200 would be just fine for the pastors along the Chixoy - a rapid but shallow river, that required narrow, maneuverable, and shallow bottom boats with portable, shallow draft motors on the back. The pastors along the river depended on the power boats for transportation; travel through the jungle was slow and cumbersome. Five thousand kilometers later, the river pastors who traveled for days to collect their "gift", declared it worthless and left disappointed. After that, the Guatemalan customs officials levied a tariff on the boat of $2000 US dollars just to get it out of the customs impound yard. I suppose that the corrupt officials wanted the boat for themselves. It was revenge to just let them have it – they didn't know as we did what a pile of junk the boat was. But I'm ahead of myself here...

So how did we get all the supplies to Guatemala? Well, Don Tipton, owner of the Spirit Ship, had an old school bus that he wanted to donate to a church in Guatemala City but had nobody to drive it there. Our Guatemala pastor friend had supplies to bring to Guatemala but no transportation. So now you see the connection. Don Tipton gave me $600 for gas to drive the bus to Guatemala, and away we went. But not before I took every tool imaginable with me, anticipating the need. I ended up using most of them due to the treacherous Mexican roads.

In all it was an 8-week journey fraught with 3 weeks of road dangers and continual interfacing with corrupt people. Amid it though, God was there to encourage us and use us. In particular was a 3-day ministry time at a village along the Chixoy river where the language spoken was K'iche'. Diane and I spoke in English, our pastor friend interpreted into Spanish, and another pastor interpreted into K'iche'. The village people were beautiful, and innocent, and I believe that they were touched through our ministry. While there in that village, interacting with the women, Diane became burdened to be among them, and desired to return to live with them. We also went to Almolonga, a city that had once been overrun with corruption and debauchery, but through the Gospel, became mostly saved and beautiful. God blessed their land to produce bountifully, and we saw amazingly large fruits and vegetables. We also participated there in a grand parade with thousands of native people celebrating the opening of a new, large church building. The theme of their parade was "Jesus is Lord". The indigenous ladies dressed Diane in their native costume, and she felt privileged to walk in the parade with them. We learned a lot on this journey to Guatemala, of what to do, and what not to do.

I'm grateful that we returned at all, some didn't - burned out, crashed, vehicles were visible along the roadway.

GUATEMALA

Guatemala and Gunshots

In November 2000, I met a woman named Irma from Guatemala while in Los Angeles. During that time, the Lord radically touched her son when I prayed for and ministered to him over the phone. He had been very lost, but after that prayer, God moved in his life in a powerful way. He received Jesus and threw out all his pornography, broke up with his girlfriend, and surrendered himself to the Lord. He began hungering for the things of God and wanted to live a holy life. Around that same time, a group of intercessors were preparing to go to Guatemala, and they invited me to accompany them on their trip. Irma was part of the intercessor team.

I said, "Lord, if You want me to go on this trip, you'll make the way for me." We live by faith, and trust God to supply our needs and provision.

That very night, I received a phone call from the son of Irma. He told me, "The Lord put it on my heart to pay for your ticket." And just like that, God made the way for me.

At the time, though, I didn't have many clothes. I rarely went shopping, and the clothes I wore were mostly donated clothes from our clothes ministry. I prayed, "Lord, I really need something to wear for this trip." I took a train to Los Angeles where I would be flying out with the group a couple of days later, and a new friend, Diana, picked me up.

We visited a large church—many of the women going on the trip were members there. As I walked in, a woman approached me and said, "You're the one. The Lord told me to take you to the mall and get you whatever you need—whatever you want." I was stunned. She bought everything I needed for the trip. The incredible part? She wasn't even planning to attend church that day. She had been at home when the Lord told her to go to the church and look for a woman. That woman was me.

That trip to Guatemala was deeply anointed. I fasted for 7 days straight and never felt hungry as we went from house to house, place to place praying for people and for freedom to come into lives. I was so thankful—for the provision, for the obedience of those who heard God's voice, and for the opportunity to go and serve.

Sometimes when traveling, we go into very dangerous places, where our lives could be at risk. In Mexico, we were chased by the state police and our lives were in danger there, but God brought us through that one.

But in going on this particular trip, I told my husband, "You know what? If I must give my life for the sake of God's kingdom—to go and share—then I'm willing." I arrived in Guatemala with a group of ladies and ministered for several days. The final days that we were there, we were in an area that was very dangerous. We had just arrived at someone's house in a ghetto area, and someone tried to push in the door, and we began to hear gunshots.

Our hosts said, "Oh, they're probably here to get you, Diane, because they know you're an American." All the ladies that I traveled with were Hispanic, from Guatemala or Mexico, I was the only one who had fair skin. I began to feel a lot of fear. I called Jamie, and thank God, I was able to get through.

Jamie said, "Remember, Diane, you said you would give your life if you needed to." Sometimes we say things, and God puts us to the test. Believe me, I felt a lot of fear.

I didn't realize that fear was in me. I remember all night long, the gunshots. I told them, "Call the police." They said, "We can't, they are afraid to come in this area." The Lord tested me.

The next morning, when we woke up, we thanked God for keeping us safe throughout the night. We later found out we had been in the middle of a gang fight. I only had two days left before heading home, and I couldn't wait to leave. During that time, God revealed areas of weakness in me—places where fear had taken root and where I wasn't fully trusting Him. He showed me that I needed Him to remove that fear and teach me to always trust Him.

I learned one thing, be very careful what you say. God brought me through this process, and I feel more prepared now than I did then. I hadn't realized how much fear was inside me.

That was the lesson that God taught me.

Venezuela

In January 1995, while living at the village in Mexico, we had an invitation from a Venezuelan pastor who had stayed at Sommer Haven for a while, to come to Venezuela and teach about the Isaiah 58 vision. A missionary couple from Sommer Haven came to Mexico to keep the ministry running at the village while Jamie and I packed our things and children and drove the 10 hours back to Sommer Haven. Within a week we were in South America and our children stayed at Sommer Haven and at a related ministry center in Oregon. It was always so amazing how the Lord made provisions for us. We had no salary or regular income of any kind, but people who knew us were moved to put money in our hand for our trip.

Jamie and I were in Venezuela for about 6 weeks. We ministered in churches, shared the vision of Isaiah 58 in meetings, visited many homes, and prayed. We were housed in a prayer compound located in the downtown district of our host's city. It was a rough area, but we did not feel uncomfortable.

I'll share just one episode of our time there.

A local pastor came one day to visit our host pastor asking for his assistance with a serious situation. The visiting pastor had a relative cousin who had lived many years in Colorado but somehow had lost her mind and the family tried everything to help the young lady to no avail. Their last resort was to bring the girl back to her homeland of Venezuela to their cousin pastor to see if he could provide spiritual help because the family of the girl suspected demonic activity as the root cause. The next day, Monday morning, the family brought the girl to the prayer compound where Jamie and I stayed. She really was out of her mind. Our host pastor decided that the girl couldn't be helped, but I asked the pastor to give us some time with her. The family agreed to pick up the girl on Friday afternoon because the next day, Saturday, they were all flying away to another place in Venezuela where they lived. The girl stayed with us at the compound all week, and I slept next to her praying for her through the night, and in the day Jamie and I had long prayer and deliverance sessions with her. By Friday afternoon when the family came back for her, the girl was much better, by Friday night she was better yet and, we heard later, on Saturday morning she was almost normal.

We never saw her again but did hear that she became completely normal, married, became a mother and lived life. The last information we heard about her was that she had a very vague memory of an American couple who prayed for her deliverance, restoration and mental healing.

We returned home from Venezuela to Sommer Haven and then to our village in Mexico in March 1995 and returned to Venezuela a final time in November of that year for a two-week time of revival in a stadium and general ministry.

After that, in December 1995, we went back to the village in Mexico for the last time, said our farewells, moved our belongings and vehicles, and went through the next door that opened to us at Kings Ranch in Kings County, California. We have been there now for almost 30 years.

CHIHUAHUA
MEXICO

CHIHUAHUA
MEXICO

CHIHUAHUA
MEXICO

CHIHUAHUA MEXICO

TARAHUMARA
INDIANS MEXICO

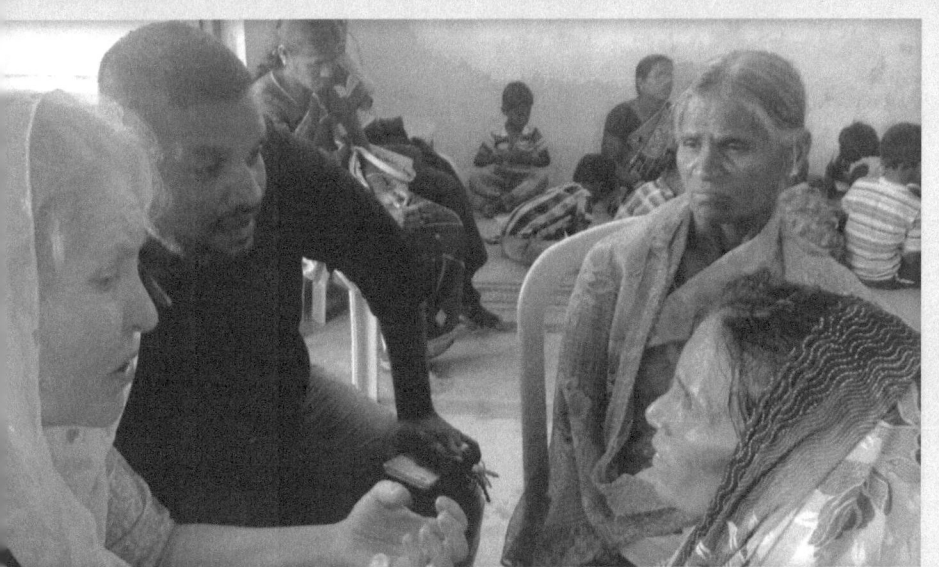

INDIA

INDIA

India

In 2012, in a church meeting near Hanford, a minister whom I had never met before, prophesied to me that God was going to bring India to our ministry. Little did I know that bringing India to me would result in India bringing me to it. I was deeply stirred by his words and shortly after, we began meeting different Indian ministers and Christians.

One person we met was our dear Sister Minni, who began visiting us frequently. In early 2014 Minni brought her 78-year-old mother from India to live with her in San Jose. Minni's mother, otherwise known as "Mama", a wonderful woman of God and evangelist, found fellowship with us at Kings Ranch and would stay with us for weeks at a time

engaging in fellowship, prayer, intercession and personal ministry. Mama passed on to glory in 2016. The story of the glory of God in her hospital room, and the visions that were seen, and the heavenly host that manifested when her spirit departed, is an amazing story, but must wait for another time to be told.

However, the burden of India, the mantle of Mama, afterwards came upon both me and Minni. Two years later, in April 2018, during an outdoor worship event at Kings Ranch, the Spirit of the Lord laid me low onto the ground and showed me that I was to accompany Minni to India, who was traveling there the following month. After lots of preparation, in early May, we flew to Chennai, India.

In our 4 weeks of ministry in India we ministered in several churches, prayed with people in remote areas, visited homes, and helped with an Isaiah 58 food outreach to the "Untouchables" - gypsy people living in slum areas who are the lowest caste of people and who are not schooled.

Minni's brother arranged for us to meet Pastor Sesaron and his parents, who are pastors, who conduct outreaches in villages and streets and who disciple in their church. We ministered with them in different places. Sesaron adopted me as his 2nd mother, started calling me "Mom", and gladly became my interpreter everywhere we went. We continue to send monthly support to their ministry today, 7 years later.

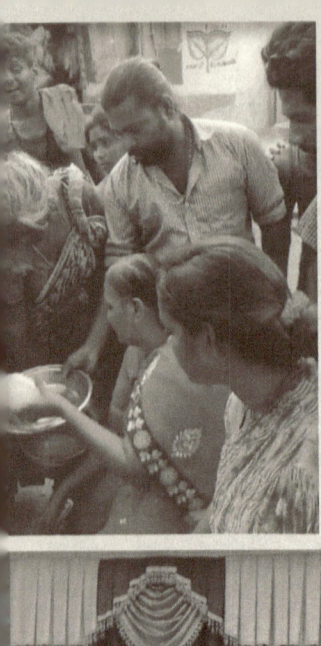

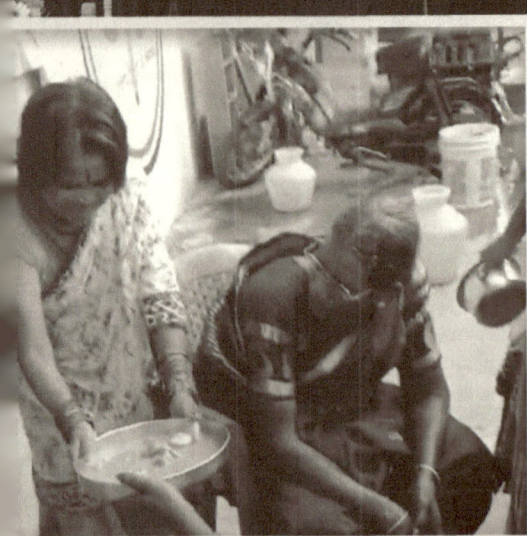

Breakthrough in India

Jamie and I were invited by Dr. Rev. J. Sam Jebadurai, the founder of Elim Glorious Revival Church and a well-known, highly respected pastor, to his church in India. Brother Sam (as He was affectionately called in India) was disappointed that Jamie was not able to come. He had  expected him to preach that morning and had asked me to share something and pray for his congregation.

We came to know Brother Sam in about 2014 at a conference in San Jose on one of his annual trips to the United States. He would minister to Tamil speaking congregations around the country, and although he was more comfortable speaking his native Tamil, he could speak English quite well too. Brother Sam was an amazing man of God who preached with revelation and power who also walked in meekness and, as of 2016, had completed the assignments given him by the Lord. He had to overcome physical infirmities that left him partially crippled but his faithful endurance in all things gained him the nature of Jesus.

Brother Sam felt like a father to me. He wasn't well in May 2018 when I stayed with his family, and just a few months later, he passed away.

But that Sunday, standing at his pulpit, I could feel the presence of God. Brother Sam had just preached and then invited me to share a few words with the congregation. I offered a brief testimony and some words of encouragement, and I felt led to blow the shofar to shift the atmosphere. That morning, I blew it with all my might.

Since Brother Sam had asked me to pray for his people, I invited them to come forward for prayer.

At first, a few came forward, and as I placed my hands on them, God's power flowed and brought deliverance in their lives. Many were crying, some were shouting, liberty and freedom and self-worth and love flowed into them. The altar area began flooding with those seeking liberty and a newness of life that Christ was graciously pouring out upon them.

What God did that day was truly beautiful. As I stretched out my hand toward one man, before I even touched him, God did. He fell to the floor, weeping in God's presence, receiving the freedom of Christ. Many others also fell to the ground, weeping—overwhelmed by the power of God. Afterwards, Brother Sam shared how deeply blessed he was to witness his people receiving freedom and life.

I finished that day with much gratitude to God.

In the days that followed, as ministry continued in India, I reflected on my 57 years of life, and I knew that God's great grace alone had brought me this far. I shouldn't be here. By all accounts I should be dead, drugged, or wasted. As I thought back to my earliest days, to the sorrow of my childhood, the rebellion of my teen years, and the final surrender to Christ, I saw the thread of divine destiny that had been woven into my life. And it became clear - there was a purpose, and it had a beginning.

> "The Spirit of the Lord God is upon me; because the Lord hath anointed me to preach good tidings unto the meek; he hath sent me to bind up the brokenhearted, to proclaim liberty to the captives, and the opening of the prison to them that are bound;"
>
> — Isaiah 61:1

EL SALVADOR

EL SALVADOR

El Salvador

In 2024, I was praying and asking the Lord what my next assignment would be. I heard very clearly: El Salvador. That very morning, my dear friend Cenia texted me, asking, 'When are you coming to El Salvador?' I immediately felt a strong confirmation—that it was the Lord speaking. I searched online and found a very reasonably priced ticket. Amazingly, my daughter-in-law's father works for that airline and offered to help by waiving my luggage fees. It felt as though God was already preparing the way ahead of me.

In October, I arrived in El Salvador, without any agenda in my mind. Once there, though, doors for ministry just began opening, I didn't try to force anything on my own but connections with other Christians and pastors just came to me and it was evident that His hand was guiding my steps and the experience truly felt like a divine appointment.

One day, we stopped at a gas station for coffee, and I noticed a Bible at the cash register. To me, that was a sign the owners were Christian. As we sat there, I saw a group of women in the next room and assumed it was some kind of training. Then a man walked in, also carrying a Bible, and we struck up a conversation. My friend Cenia shared about the ministry work we'd been doing, and the man told us, 'I'm here to minister to these women. They've recently been released from prison and are now part of a rehabilitation program. Once they complete it, they're given a chance to work here at the gas station." The Lord opened a door that day allowing me to share His love with that group of women - each one broken, each one searching. As I spoke to them about how God's love heals the brokenhearted, His presence filled the room. The women began to weep, and it was clear that the Holy Spirit was moving powerfully among us.

That encounter was one of the highlights of the trip, though the entire journey was full of divine surprises. I hadn't arrived in El Salvador with an agenda, but God had one—and He moved mightily.

Later, I learned from pastors at a local church, that they'd received a prophetic word just days before my arrival: someone from the Philippines would come bearing a message from the Lord to uplift them. I had just returned from the Philippines—and, it appeared, that I was that messenger. God used me to speak a word of affirmation and prophetic encouragement over their lives, and something new was birthed in the Spirit that day. After the prayer, the pastors began to prophesy which was a new experience for them.

This journey to El Salvador reminded me once again that God's plans are often beyond our own understanding. When we step out in faith, even without a clear agenda, He is already preparing the way—opening doors, orchestrating divine appointments, and moving powerfully to bring healing and hope.

I was humbled and grateful to be used by God as a vessel for His love and encouragement, in every place where He leads. This experience reaffirmed to me that no matter how uncertain the path, God's hand is always guiding, and His Spirit is ready to lead when we say "yes."

May this testimony inspire others to listen closely to God's voice, trust His timing, and be willing to follow wherever He calls. For in His perfect plan, every step taken in faith brings forth new life, new hope, and new beginnings.

The Philippines

Over the years, we've had the honor of hosting groups from various places who came to Kings Ranch seeking renewal and a fresh touch from God. Among them were July and Edwin from the Philippines, who had settled in Los Angeles years before. They visited Kings Ranch several times, gathering for prayer, worship, and fellowship together.

July had a strong desire in her heart to return to the Philippines to establish a house of prayer, so they sold everything and went back to the Philippines.

Once there, they began the work of building a house of prayer. Friends from the United States, especially Cameron and Mariela, carried a shared vision and offered support in various ways to help bring this dream to life. They purchased property and renovated it and began hosting times of prayer with the local community.

In May 2024, Mariela and Cameron, friends of ours who introduced us to July and Edwin and who carried a strong burden to go to the Philippines, led a team on a 10-day trip to Negros Island where July and Edwin live. Jamie and I were invited to be part of the team, but Jamie declined to go due to responsibilities at home. During our stay in the Philippines, we had the opportunity to carry out outreaches and a crusade with different churches and in different areas. We saw lives being touched, hearts being stirred, and communities coming together in worship and prayer.

Each team member brought two suitcases from the USA, one of personal things and the other filled with children's clothes and supplies. We were able to distribute the supplies to villages, and it became a fruitful time in God's presence. We ministered to children, prayed over women and families, and witnessed God moving powerfully, especially through Cameron and Mariela's worship and ministry. Their daughter Sofia joined the trip as well and helped lead worship. She was only 13 years old, yet he carried a deep burden to support the mission—handcrafting bracelets to raise funds so she could provide 100 notebooks and pens for the children. We distributed these gifts to children in a remote mountain village, and their joy and gratitude were unforgettable.

July shared something special with me - she had placed a fountain in her prayer room as a symbol of her connection to our ministry. It was a beautiful reminder of the spiritual bond that continues between us.

As I reflect on all these years—on the journeys, the friendships, and the faithfulness of God—I am reminded that ministry is never just about one place or one moment. It is about the connections we build, the seeds we sow, and the rivers of life that flow from one heart to another, across oceans and cultures.

PHILIPPINES
OFFICE OF THE MAYOR
CITY OF TALISAY

PHILIPPINES

JAPAN

ZAMBIA

ZAMBIA

- Zambia

By James Profet

In August 2010, Deborah Webb, Jamie, and I flew to Johannesburg, South Africa, to meet with Sister Felistus Nawa and attend a four-day African Women's Aglow conference before flying to Lusaka, Zambia, for the remainder of our three-week trip. It was our first time on African soil and our first time seeing Felistus in three years.

Felistus, a Zambian national, pastor, and evangelist, grew up in villages on the rural outskirts of Lusaka, living in primitive grass huts. She experienced poverty, ignorance, and sin, but after a life-changing encounter with Jesus Christ—while at the point of death and descending into hell—she cried out, acknowledged her sins, repented of each one, and found mercy unto salvation. During that experience, she promised the Lord that if He would grant her mercy, she would serve Him always. The Lord brought her spirit back from the gateway of hell and restored her to life.

Felistus kept her word and often traveled barefoot over great distances to proclaim Christ. On one occasion, a mother came to Felistus holding her recently deceased baby and said, "I have heard that your God is a God of power. My baby has just died—bring him back to life." Though hesitant to accept the request, Felistus entrusted herself to God and prayed for hours. Eventually, the child's breath returned, and, as Elijah did with the Shunammite woman, Felistus handed the living child back to his mother.

We first came to know Felistus in May 2000, when she was in America for the first time. A stranger saw her at a church in Los Angeles and invited her to a missionary conference he was organizing at King's Ranch, our ministry. Upon meeting her, our hearts were instantly knit with Felistus, and we introduced her to many people who supported her financially—both for her mission work and her personal living needs. After she returned to Zambia in June 2000, due to her primitive living conditions, we had no communication with her for five years.

In 2005, she was able to contact us again and came to the United States for a Women's Aglow conference. We brought her to California, where she stayed with us for six months, and together we ministered in many churches and meetings. She returned to America once more for the 2007 Women's Aglow conference and stayed with us for two months. When the U.S. Consulate in Zambia denied her visa renewal in 2009, we decided to travel to Zambia to see her.

While in Zambia, Felistus took us to various areas where we ministered and prayed for the people. During one outreach in a densely populated compound, she showed the *Jesus Film* to a large crowd. After the showing, we prayed for salvation and restoration with all who desired it. It was quite unusual to see "Jesus" in the film speaking Nyanja, the local dialect!

We had many experiences with Felistus during our three-week visit to Zambia. When the time came to return home, we sadly parted ways and have not seen Felistus in person since. However, now that Zambia has a developed cellular network, we stay in frequent contact with her for prayer and to provide financial support for her ongoing ministry and outreaches throughout Zambia.

About the Author

 Diane Profet is a passionate minister, prayer warrior, and global servant dedicated to uplifting the lives of those in need. With a heart rooted in compassion and a calling to serve, she has spent many years traveling around the world - offering hope and faith to groups, churches and individuals facing hardship. Whether through hands-on outreach, mentoring, or intercessory prayer, Diane brings light and love wherever she goes.

Her mission is simple: to remain deeply passionate about knowing God and spending time ministering. Even if she just reaches one person, to Diane, it's completely worth it. She truly understands the impact someone connected to God can have.

Diane and her husband Jamie Profet have directed Kings Ranch in Hanford, California for 30 years.

A special thanks to Teresa Skinner.

www.ingramcontent.com/pod-product-compliance
Lightning Source LLC
Chambersburg PA
CBHW031309120626
46554CB00001BA/344